UNDERSTANDING
THE
SIDDUR

UNDERSTANDING
THE
SIDDUR

by SHIRLEY STERN

KTAV PUBLISHING HOUSE, INC.

TABLE OF CONTENTS

To the Teacher

The goal of *Understanding the Siddur* is to encourage students to pray, to teach them how to pray, to explore why we pray, and to develop familiarity with the format and procedure of the various services as well as with the Hebrew prayers. Throughout the book there are comments and descriptions aimed at making the prayers more meaningful. Values clarification techniques are used to provide the students with an emotional framework that will, it is hoped, lead to commitment. Skill exercises are included to reinforce learning and make it fun.

A great deal of supplementary material has been included along with the prayers. We have the students for so short a time in religious school that every effort should be made to teach as much as we can and to utilize every precious moment. I have, therefore, included extensive "enrichment" material, including lessons from the Midrash, Chasidic parables, Talmudic and Mishnaic observations, Biblical references, historical and philosophical materials, and Hebrew vocabulary. The words in the Hebrew vocabulary are found in the prayers but in most cases would also be useful or familiar to the students in the context of modern conversational Hebrew. It is not necessary for the students to memorize all the words, but they should learn to recognize them, since they are used in both modern Hebrew and the prayers.

A word about the translations. They were composed specifically with young readers in mind. I did not try to be poetic but instead presented them in unstilted language that the children will find meaningful and appealing. Although my goal was not to give word-for-word translations, most of my English versions are fairly close to the original Hebrew. In regard to gender-related terms, however, I have sought to abide by the current educational practice of avoiding "sexist" language wherever possible, even though this means in some cases that Hebrew words or phrases cannot be translated in the most obvious and familiar ways.

In order to derive the greatest benefit from this text, it should be utilized along with the suggestions and methodology in the Teacher's Guide. In that way the students will be provided with a total learning experience.

BEFORE WE BEGIN

The young boy sat beside his parents in the synagogue. All around him sat the members of the congregation—his friends, his parents' friends, and many others whom he did not know. All held their prayerbooks before their eyes and prayed the words of the service..

But the young boy did not pray. He did not know the prayers. He had just begun to study at Hebrew school. All he had learned so far were the letters of the Hebrew alphabet—the alefbet.

The young boy longed to pray with the others. There was so much for which to thank God. There were joys and fears he wanted to share. There was love and gratitude he wanted to express. He knew that all these feelings were expressed in the prayers. If only he could pray with the others.

At last, the young boy could contain himself no longer. He began to pray silently to himself—not in the words of the prayerbook, but in his own words. "O God," he prayed, "I would like to thank you for the beauty of this world I live in. I would like to tell you of my fears and joys. I would like to share my hopes and dreams. But I do not know the prayers. I only know the letters of the alefbet. But you know the prayers. God, please listen as I recite the alphabet, and please, won't you put the letters together into the proper words and prayers?"

And the boy began to recite silently, "Alef, bet, gimmel, dalet, hay, vav . . ."

—Chasidic Story

Since time began, men and women have longed to express their fears, their hopes, and their gratitude to their gods. In primitive times people believed that forces in nature that they could not understand controlled their destiny. So they worshipped the sun, the moon, the stars, the trees, or animals. Later in human history, people carved idols from stone or wood to represent their gods. These gods often had strange shapes with many arms, legs, or heads. Temples were built to house the idols, and the faithful came there to worship them. Often a tribe or a nation had its own god which the people believed protected them from harm and evil.

The Jews were the first people to develop the idea of one God. They worshipped a God whom they could not see or control. They believed in a God who was the master of the universe, and who ruled the world with justice and love. In those days the Jews lived in their own country, the land of Israel. As was the custom at that time, they built a beautiful temple where they worshipped God by bringing sacrifices. The Temple, or Bet Hamikdash (Holy House), was in the city of Jerusalem, the capital of the land of Israel.

A reconstruction of the interior of the Temple in Jerusalem.

The religious rituals in the Temple were presided over by a group of specially trained priests. They were assisted in their religious duties by another special group called Levites. Both the priests called Cohanim and the Levites inherited their positions and dedicated their lives to the service of God. They had to know many rules and laws in order to perform the sacrifical rituals, which could take place only in the Bet Hamikdash.

But a time came when God could no longer be worshipped by bringing sacrifices to the Temple in Jerusalem. In 586 B.C.E. Jerusalem was conquered by the Babylonians and the Temple was destroyed. Many Jews were deported from Israel to Babylonia.

A reconstruction of the clothing of the Cohanim.

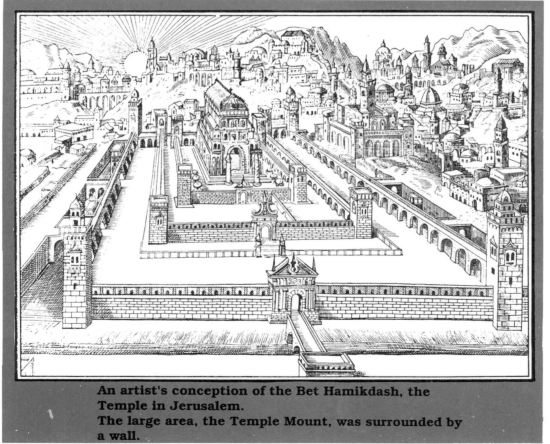

An artist's conception of the Bet Hamikdash, the Temple in Jerusalem.
The large area, the Temple Mount, was surrounded by a wall.

This was a very crucial moment in the history of Judaism. Most ancient religions were very closely connected to a particular country or place. The gods could only be worshipped in the homeland of their worshippers; they were believed to be powerful in the homeland of their worshippers but not necessarily in other areas. If the worshippers settled somewhere else, they adopted the religion of their new home, and their old religion died out.

When the Jews were forced to move from Israel to Babylonia, and no longer had a central shrine where they could practice the rituals of their religion, Judaism was faced with a serious threat. Unlike many other ancient religions, however, it survived these adverse historical circumstances. Judaism did not die. First of all, the God of Judaism was not limited to a particular place. Second, the Jews in Babylonia developed a "portable religion," a way to worship God that did not depend on a specific location or shrine. The Jews in Babylonia did this by meeting in small groups to study Judaism and worship God. From this beginning developed the synagogue as we know it in our time, a place for Jews to worship God, to study, and to meet to discuss common problems. The Temple had to be in Jerusalem, but synagogues could be anywhere. By developing the synagogue, Jews had a place to worship no matter where they lived.

Through the years the prayer service used in the synagogue changed and developed. Many great Jewish poets and authors wrote beautiful prayers in Hebrew expressing their love for God and their devotion to the ideals of Judaism. These were added to the worship service. Special ceremonies also became part

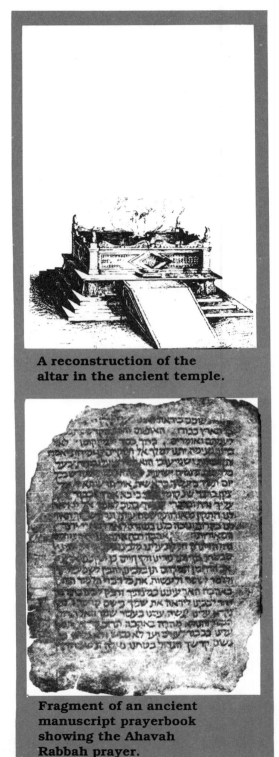

A reconstruction of the altar in the ancient temple.

Fragment of an ancient manuscript prayerbook showing the Ahavah Rabbah prayer.

of the service, as did the reading of the Torah. Music was an important part of the service. Many of the prayers had their own special melodies, which varied from place to place. Sometimes all the worshippers participated in singing the prayers, while at other times, the service was sung by a specially trained chazan (cantor). The act of praying is sometimes called *davening*, from the Yiddish word *daven*, "to pray."

When the worship service had developed a definite form and order, it was written down in a prayerbook called the Siddur. The word Siddur means "order," and this name was applied to the prayerbook because it gives us the "order" of prayers for the entire year. Not all Jews worship from the same Siddur. There is a Sephardic Siddur for Mediterranean Jews, an Ashkenazic Siddur for European Jews, a Conservative Siddur for Conservative Jews, and a Reform Siddur called *Gates of Prayer* for Reform Jews. But although the Siddurim differ from each other in form and in the amount of Hebrew used, the basic prayers and the format of the service remain more or less the same.

Page from an old Siddur published in the 1800's.

PRAYER VOCABULARY	
Synagogue, Temple	בֵּית כְּנֶסֶת
Cantor	חַזָּן
Rabbi	רַב
Holy Temple	בֵּית הַמִּקְדָּשׁ
Jerusalem	יְרוּשָׁלַיִם
Hebrew	עִבְרִית
English	אַנְגְּלִית
Land of Israel	אֶרֶץ יִשְׂרָאֵל
Reading of the Torah	קְרִיאַת הַתּוֹרָה
Siddur	סִדּוּר

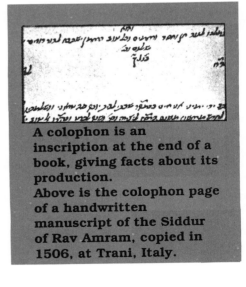

**A colophon is an inscription at the end of a book, giving facts about its production.
Above is the colophon page of a handwritten manuscript of the Siddur of Rav Amram, copied in 1506, at Trani, Italy.**

FOCUS ON THE CONCEPT: KAVANAH

The poems and phrases of the Siddur are very beautiful and very moving. But even beautiful poetry is not prayer until it is read or spoken by someone who is "praying." It is only when it is said by someone who is trying to feel close to God that it becomes prayer.

Jews have a word for the special feeling that changes a beautiful poem or phrase into a prayer. It is *kavanah*. Loosely translated, kavanah means "sincerity." But the concept really means much more than sincerity. It is the spirit and intensity with which we pray.

It is our feeling of love for God and for our fellow Jews. It is our expression of our innermost fears, hopes, and dreams. "All commandments (mitzvot), "our ancient rabbis said, "must be done with kavanah." But they did not explain exactly what kavanah was. They left it as a feeling to be experienced individually by each Jew who participates in a mitzvah or prayer.

It is important when we pray, not only to know the words of the prayer, but to concentrate on the thoughts and feelings behind the prayer—to pray with kavanah.

PRAYER VOCABULARY	
Commandment of God	מִצְוָה
Prayer	תְּפִלָּה
Poem	פִּיוּט
Sincerity	כַּוָּנָה

14

The Siddur, or prayerbook, contains the order of the service. The first Siddur was compiled by Amram Gaon in the ninth century, over a thousand years ago. Since that time there have been many versions of the prayerbook. There is an Ashkenazic Siddur and a Sephardic Siddur. Jews in Italy have their own prayerbook, as do Jews in North Africa, while in the United States a number of different prayerbooks are used. Orthodox, Conservative, Reconstructionist, and Reform Jews each have their own version of the Siddur.

In the early days of Conservative Judaism, nearly a century ago, Conservative and Orthodox congregations used the same Siddur. After a while, however, Conservative Jews began to feel the need for a prayerbook of their own.

The first Conservative prayerbook, a Machzor for Passover, Shavuot, and Sukkot, was published in 1927. It was replaced in 1946 by the *Sabbath and Festival Prayer Book*

Title page of the Silverman prayerbook published by the Rabbinical Assembly and the United Synagogue.

published by the Rabbinical Assembly, the organization of Conservative rabbis, and the United Synagogue, the organization of Conservative congregations.

The *Sabbath and Festival Prayer Book* is often called the Silverman prayerbook in honor of Rabbi Morris J. Silverman who prepared the original manuscript. It met many needs of the growing Conservative movement. The English translations in this Siddur made it easier for worshippers to understand the service.

Some of the traditional prayers were revised so as to harmonize them with the Conservative philosophy. For example, traditional prayerbooks have always expressed a wish for the restoration of the sacrifices that used to take place in the Holy Temple in Jerusalem. Conservative Judaism, however, does not expect a restoration of animal sacrifice. The Silverman prayerbook does not say that the sacrifices should begin again but only asks God to *remember* how the sacrifices were offered by our ancestors. We pray that God will grant us the same spirit of devotion as was expressed at those ancient services.

The Silverman prayerbook is still widely used, but some Conservative congregations prefer other books, such as the Siddur compiled by Rabbi Ben Zion Bokser (1957). Similarly, while some congregations use the Silverman Machzor for Rosh Hashanah and Yom Kippur (1951), and others use Bokser's, many have adopted the new Machzor published by the Rabbinical Assembly in 1972. For weekday services, Conservative congregations generally use the Rabbinical Assembly's Weekday Prayerbook (1961).

Since the Conservative movement encompasses a wide range of religious beliefs and practices, it was difficult to develop a prayerbook acceptable to everyone. However a committee of Conservative scholars prepared a new Siddur called *Sim Shalom*. Building on the previous Conservative prayerbooks, it is the first comprehensive Siddur for all occasions—Shabbat, festivals, and weekdays. It is published officially by the Rabbinical Assembly in association with the United Synagogue of America.

PRAYER VOCABULARY	
Hebrew	עִבְרִית
English	אַנְגְּלִית
Ashkenazi	אַשְׁכְּנַזִי
Sephardi	סְפָרַדִי
Prayerbook	סִדּוּר
Prayerbook for the holidays	מַחֲזוֹר

תְּפִלַּת שַׁבָּת
SHABBAT PRAYERS

SHABBAT שַׁבָּת

On Shabbat, Jews pray both at home and in the synagogue. Many families begin Shabbat at home by lighting and blessing candles, and reciting Kiddush and Hamotzi. Often the home service also includes the singing of the hymn Shalom Aleichem and other Shabbat songs, or Zmirot.

Shabbat, the day of rest, is ushered in with the lighting of the candles.

After dinner, many families attend late Friday evening Shabbat services. Although this was an innovation introduced by Reform Jews, many Conservative and some Orthodox synagogues now hold a late Friday evening service. These services usually include a sermon by the rabbi as well as the traditional prayers. Sometimes candles are lit and blessed and Kiddush is recited in the synagogue as well as at home. Often the service is followed by an Oneg Shabbat, a social hour where friends who have not seen each other all week can meet and enjoy each other's company.

The Shabbat morning service includes the reading of the Torah as well as a prayer service. The Torah is divided into weekly portions, one to be read each Shabbat. The reading of the Torah is preceded and followed by special blessings recited by members of the congregation. If there is a Bar or Bat Mitzvah, the

A special volume called a Tikkun is used to practice reading the Torah correctly. In the Tikkun the right-hand column includes vowel points and cantillation notes. In the left-hand column the same section is printed just as it appears in the Torah scroll. The word Tikkun means "correction."

boy or girl being honored participates in the Torah service. After the Torah reading, a portion from the Prophets is read. This is also preceded and followed by special blessings.

The concluding service for Shabbat is the Havdalah, or "Separation" service. This ceremony ends Shabbat and sets it aside from the rest of the week. Havdalah is a very beautiful ceremony which may be observed either in the synagogue or at home.

PRAYER VOCABULARY

Weekly Torah portion	סִדְרָה
Bar Mitzvah	בַּר מִצְוָה
Bat Mitzvah	בַּת מִצְוָה
Kiddush	קִדּוּשׁ
Torah	תּוֹרָה
Shabbat morning service	שַׁחֲרִית
Havdalah	הַבְדָּלָה
Celebration of the Sabbath	עֹנֶג שַׁבָּת
Synagogue	בֵּית כְּנֶסֶת
Shabbat songs	זְמִירוֹת
Blessing over bread	הַמּוֹצִיא
Additional service for Shabbat and holy days	מוּסָף

SHABBAT AT HOME

*Two angels visit every Jewish home on Shabbat eve—
a good angel and an evil one. If the angels come into
a home and see that the candles have been lit, the table set for Shabbat, and the family gathered peace-
fully and happily to observe Shabbat, the good angel
is very happy and says, "May it be like this every
Shabbat." The evil angel, sadly and against his will,
must say "Amen."*

*But if the angels find no preparation for Shabbat,
if the members of the family are fighting among themselves, then the evil angel is very happy and says,
"May it be like this every Shabbat." The good angel
must sadly and against his will say "Amen."*

—Talmudic Legend

SHABBAT AT HOME   שַׁבָּת בַּבַּיִת

Shabbat begins at home with the lighting of candles. Lighting ceremonial lights to start the celebration of Shabbat is an ancient ceremony and was already well known in the second century C.E.

The mother of the family ushers in Shabbat and sets it apart from the rest of the week by lighting the candles and reciting the blessing. Sometimes other members of the family participate in the candle-lighting ceremony.

PRAYER VOCABULARY

Blessing	בְּרָכָה
Sabbath	שַׁבָּת
Candle (Candles)	נֵר (נֵרוֹת)
Candlelighting	הַדְלָקַת הַנֵּרוֹת

The blessing that is said tells us that observing the commandment of lighting candles for Shabbat makes us holy or special.

Blessed is the Eternal	בָּרוּךְ אַתָּה יְיָ,
our God, ruler of the world,	אֱלֹהֵינוּ מֶלֶךְ הָעוֹלָם,
who made us holy by the Mitzvot	אֲשֶׁר קִדְּשָׁנוּ בְּמִצְוֹתָיו,
by commanding us to light candles on Shabbat.	וְצִוָּנוּ לְהַדְלִיק נֵר שֶׁל־שַׁבָּת.

COMMANDING US TO LIGHT CANDLES ON SHABBAT   וְצִוָּנוּ לְהַדְלִיק נֵר שֶׁל־שַׁבָּת

The great Jewish philosopher Maimonides taught that lighting Shabbat lights is such an important ceremony that if a family has no money for food and must beg, its members also have a religious duty to beg for the money to buy oil to light Shabbat lights.

Often the lighting of Shabbat candles is preceded by an act of Zedakah. Many families have charity boxes into which coins are placed every week before Shabbat begins.

PRAYER VOCABULARY

Candlelighting	הַדְלָקַת הַנֵּרוֹת
Blessed is the Eternal	בָּרוּךְ אַתָּה יְיָ
Ruler of the world	מֶלֶךְ הָעוֹלָם
Who made us holy	אֲשֶׁר קִדְּשָׁנוּ
Candle (Candles)	נֵר (נֵרוֹת)

22

The Shabbat meal begins with Kiddush recited over a cup of wine. The Kiddush is a prayer which expresses the holiness of Shabbat. Wine is a symbol of joy and celebration. In ancient times every festive meal began with the drinking of a cup of wine. Usually the wine for Kiddush is placed in a beautifully decorated silver goblet called a Kiddush Cup. The head of the family recites the prayer and all the members of the family sip the wine. In some families it is the custom for each person at the table to recite the Kiddush individually.

It was evening and morning on the sixth day.

וַיְהִי־עֶרֶב, וַיְהִי־בֹקֶר, יוֹם הַשִּׁשִּׁי.

The heavens and the earth and all that was within them had been completed.

וַיְכֻלּוּ הַשָּׁמַיִם וְהָאָרֶץ וְכָל־צְבָאָם.

God finished all the work of creation by the seventh day.

וַיְכַל אֱלֹהִים בַּיּוֹם הַשְּׁבִיעִי, מְלַאכְתּוֹ אֲשֶׁר עָשָׂה,

And God rested on the seventh day

וַיִּשְׁבֹּת בַּיּוֹם הַשְּׁבִיעִי,

from doing all the work of creation.

מִכָּל מְלַאכְתּוֹ אֲשֶׁר עָשָׂה.

And God blessed the seventh day

וַיְבָרֶךְ אֱלֹהִים אֶת־יוֹם הַשְּׁבִיעִי,

and made it holy,

וַיְקַדֵּשׁ אֹתוֹ,

because on it God had rested from

כִּי בוֹ שָׁבַת מִכָּל מְלַאכְתּוֹ,

all the work of creation.

אֲשֶׁר בָּרָא אֱלֹהִים לַעֲשׂוֹת.

Blessed is the Eternal

    our God, ruler of the world,

    the creator of the fruit of the vine.

בָּרוּךְ אַתָּה יְיָ,

אֱלֹהֵינוּ מֶלֶךְ הָעוֹלָם,

בּוֹרֵא פְּרִי הַגָּפֶן.

Kiddush can also be recited over challah.

Blessed is the Eternal

    our God, ruler of the world,

    who brings forth bread (food)

    from the earth.

בָּרוּךְ אַתָּה יְיָ,

אֱלֹהֵינוּ מֶלֶךְ הָעוֹלָם,

הַמּוֹצִיא לֶחֶם

מִן הָאָרֶץ.

PRAYER VOCABULARY	
Making holy	קָדוּשׁ
A blessing	בְּרָכָה
The creator of	בּוֹרֵא
The fruit of the vine	פְּרִי הַגָּפֶן
Who brings forth bread	הַמּוֹצִיא לֶחֶם
From the earth	מִן הָאָרֶץ
Challah (Sabbath bread)	חַלָּה
Wine	יַיִן

Blessed is the Eternal

    our God, ruler of the world,

      who made us holy by the mitzvot and loved us.

God lovingly gave us the holy Shabbat,

    which recalls the act of creation.

It is the most important day

    of holy gathering, a reminder of the exodus from Egypt.

You have chosen us and made us holy,

    among all people,

    and You have lovingly given us

      Your holy Shabbat.

Blessed is the Eternal,

    who makes Shabbat holy.

בָּרוּךְ אַתָּה יְיָ,

אֱלֹהֵינוּ מֶלֶךְ הָעוֹלָם,

אֲשֶׁר קִדְּשָׁנוּ בְּמִצְוֹתָיו וְרָצָה בָנוּ.

וְשַׁבָּת קָדְשׁוֹ בְּאַהֲבָה וּבְרָצוֹן הִנְחִילָנוּ,

זִכָּרוֹן לְמַעֲשֵׂה בְרֵאשִׁית.

כִּי הוּא יוֹם תְּחִלָּה

לְמִקְרָאֵי־קֹדֶשׁ, זֵכֶר לִיצִיאַת מִצְרָיִם.

כִּי בָנוּ בָחַרְתָּ וְאוֹתָנוּ קִדַּשְׁתָּ

מִכָּל הָעַמִּים.

וְשַׁבַּת קָדְשְׁךָ

בְּאַהֲבָה וּבְרָצוֹן הִנְחַלְתָּנוּ.

בָּרוּךְ אַתָּה יְיָ, מְקַדֵּשׁ הַשַּׁבָּת.

A REMINDER OF THE EXODUS FROM EGYPT   זֵכֶר לִיצִיאַת מִצְרָיִם

The word Kiddush means "sanctification," or "making holy." The Kiddush proclaims the holiness of Shabbat. It also makes us aware of our historical heritage by reminding us that we were freed from slavery in Egypt.

PRAYER VOCABULARY

The act of creation	מַעֲשֵׂה בְרֵאשִׁית
A reminder of the exodus from Egypt	זֵכֶר לִיצִיאַת מִצְרָיִם
You have chosen us	כִּי בָנוּ בָחַרְתָּ
From among all peoples	מִכָּל הָעַמִּים
Your holy Shabbat	וְשַׁבַּת קָדְשְׁךָ
Who makes Shabbat holy	מְקַדֵּשׁ הַשַּׁבָּת

After the festive Shabbat meal has been eaten, a hymn of thanksgiving called Birkat Hamazon, or Grace After the Meal, is recited or sung. This prayer is very old and tells of God's kindness in providing food for all of us.

Blessed is the Eternal	בָּרוּךְ אַתָּה יְיָ,
our God, ruler of the world,	אֱלֹהֵינוּ מֶלֶךְ הָעוֹלָם,
who feeds the whole world with goodness,	הַזָּן אֶת־הָעוֹלָם כֻּלּוֹ בְּטוּבוֹ,
grace, kindness, and mercy.	בְּחֵן, בְּחֶסֶד וּבְרַחֲמִים,
God feeds all living things	הוּא נוֹתֵן לֶחֶם לְכָל־בָּשָׂר,
because God's kindness is forever.	כִּי לְעוֹלָם חַסְדּוֹ.
Because of God's great goodness	וּבְטוּבוֹ הַגָּדוֹל,
we have never been without food,	תָּמִיד לֹא־חָסַר לָנוּ
may it never be lacking,	וְאַל יֶחְסַר־לָנוּ מָזוֹן לְעוֹלָם וָעֶד.
for the sake of His great name	בַּעֲבוּר שְׁמוֹ הַגָּדוֹל
because God nourishes	כִּי הוּא אֵל זָן וּמְפַרְנֵס לַכֹּל,
and sustains all living things	וּמֵטִיב לַכֹּל,
and provides food for all the	וּמֵכִין מָזוֹן לְכָל־בְּרִיּוֹתָיו,
creatures God created.	אֲשֶׁר בָּרָא.
Blessed is the Eternal	בָּרוּךְ אַתָּה יְיָ,
who feeds all living things.	הַזָּן אֶת־הַכֹּל.

GOD NOURISHES AND SUSTAINS ALL LIVING THINGS אֵל זָן וּמְפַרְנֵס לַכֹּל, וּמֵטִיב לַכֹּל

In the Birkat Hamazon we thank God not only for providing food for us but also for feeding all the other people in the world and even the animals.

Grace After the Meal is a very old prayer. It existed in the days of the Talmud and even long before that. According to the Talmud, parts of it were written by Moses, by Joshua, and by Kings David and Solomon.

Grace after the Meal	בִּרְכַּת הַמָּזוֹן
Who feeds the whole world	הַזָּן אֶת־הָעוֹלָם
And in God's great goodness	וּבְטוּבוֹ הַגָּדוֹל
And provides food	וּמֵכִין מָזוֹן
Who feeds all living things	הַזָּן אֶת־הַכֹּל

FOCUS ON: THE FIRST SHABBAT

The Bible tells the story of the first Shabbat in the Book of Genesis.

"The heaven and the earth were finished and all that was in them. And on the seventh day God completed all the work of creation. And God rested on the seventh day from doing all the work of creation.

"And God blessed the seventh day and made it holy, because it was the day that God rested from the work of creating the world."

—Genesis 2:1–3

FOCUS ON: THE SHABBAT COMMANDMENT

The fourth of the Ten Commandments is concerned with the observances of Shabbat. We are commanded as follows:

"Remember Shabbat to keep it holy. You may labor for six days and do all your work. But the seventh day is Shabbat for the Eternal, your God. You may not do any work on it—not you or your son or daughter, or your servants, or your animals or any stranger that is within your home. For in six days the Eternal, made heaven and earth, the sea and all that is in them.

Wood engraving of the Ten Commandments.

And God rested on the seventh day and made it holy."

—Exodus 20:8–11

28

LEARNING MORE ABOUT: SHABBAT LAMPS

In our homes Shabbat begins with the lighting of Shabbat candles. But candles were not always used to usher in Shabbat. In earlier times an oil lamp was used for this ceremony. In Europe a specially shaped many-branched oil lamp called a Shabbat lamp was used. We know that these lamps were used as early as the middle of the seventeenth century, because a Dutch woodcut print from that time shows a woman reciting the blessing before such a lamp. The oil lamp in the picture hangs above the table at eye level. Each of the six branches of the lamp contains a spout for oil. In each spout is a wick to be lit. Below the lamp is a pan to catch the dripping oil.

Many other pictures show variations of the Shabbat lamp. Most of the lamps are copper or brass. Some are very elaborate, with devices for raising and lowering the lamp. The number of branches or oil spouts varies from lamp to lamp. Some have two tiers and as many as eight spouts. Many of these lamps have been preserved and can be found in Jewish museums throughout the country and in private collections.

Shabbat lamps were used until about the middle of the nineteenth century.

A Dutch woodcut showing a woman reciting the Shabbat candlelighting blessing over an oil lamp.

PRAYER VOCABULARY	
Candles	נֵרוֹת
Oil	שֶׁמֶן

29

FOCUS ON:
HEBREW WORD FAMILIES

Just as you have parents, brothers and sisters, uncles, aunts, and cousins, Hebrew words also have relatives and belong to families. Words in other languages also have relatives. For example, the English words *sit*, *sat*, and *seat* belong to the same family, and knowing the meaning of one of these words helps you figure out the meanings of the others. But in Hebrew the families are much larger, and many more words are parts of families than in most other languages.

You are already acquainted with word families if you have been studying Hebrew for a while. For example, the word סֵדֶר , the name of the Passover ritual, and the word סִדּוּר which means "prayerbook," both come from the Hebrew word for "order," because the ritual and the prayerbook both follow a set order or sequence. The word, סְדְרָה which refers to the weekly Torah portion, also belongs to this family.

In this book you will see many examples of related words. Usually the family name has three letters. We call these the "stem" or "root" letters. The family name, or "root," of סֵדֶר , סְדְרָה , סִדּוּר , and is סדר . Related words are formed by adding certain letters or vowels before or after the "root" letters. Sometimes letters or vowels are added between the "root" letters.

Knowing the "root" letters, or family name, helps you to know what the word means.

THE FRIDAY EVENING SERVICE

It is related in the Midrash that God created a mate for every living being. The male camel had a female camel for a companion; the male fish had a female fish; the male bird had a female bird; and Adam had Eve. None of God's creations would have to be alone and unloved.

But Shabbat was created without a mate. Every other day of the week had a companion. Sunday had Monday; Tuesday had Wednesday; Thursday had Friday. But Shabbat had no one. Shabbat was sad and lonely. She complained to God. "Shouldn't I have a mate?" she asked. God replied, "Do not be sad. You will have a mate too. The Jewish people will be your companion. The Jewish people will watch over you and care for you. They will love you and cherish you."

And so it was. Shabbat became the bride of the Jewish people. She was loved and cherished and watched over like a queen. To this day, Shabbat is called the Sabbath Bride and the Queen of Days.

—Genesis Rabbah

THE FRIDAY EVENING SERVICE
קַבָּלַת שַׁבָּת

The Hebrew prayers of the Friday evening service are divided into four main sections: Kabbalat Shabbat (Welcoming Shabbat); the Shema and its accompanying blessings; the Amidah (prayers of praise); and the concluding prayers.

Welcoming Shabbat	קַבָּלַת שַׁבָּת
The Shema and Its Accompanying Blessings	שְׁמַע וּבִרְכוֹתֶיהָ
The Silent Devotion	עֲמִידָה

לְכוּ נְרַנְּנָה

**Lechu Neranina is a joyous song opening the Kabba-
lat Shabbat service.**

Come, let us sing to the Eternal	לְכוּ נְרַנְּנָה לַיָי
Let us joyfully praise the Rock who saves us.	נָרִיעָה לְצוּר יִשְׁעֵנוּ:
Let us come to God in thanksgiving	נְקַדְּמָה פָנָיו בְּתוֹדָה
And with joyous songs.	בִּזְמִרוֹת נָרִיעַ לוֹ:
For God, the Eternal, is great	כִּי אֵל גָּדוֹל יְיָ
And a greater ruler than all the mighty ones,	וּמֶלֶךְ גָּדוֹל עַל־כָּל־אֱלֹהִים:
In whose hands are the depths of the earth	אֲשֶׁר בְּיָדוֹ מֶחְקְרֵי־אָרֶץ
And the peaks of the mountains.	וְתוֹעֲפוֹת הָרִים לוֹ:

COME, LET US SING TO THE ETERNAL   לְכוּ נְרַנְּנָה לַיָי

    This song of praise which opens the Friday night service is Psalm 95. It acknowledges the creative powers of God Who formed the entire universe. This song expresses the theme of Shabbat, for God's work of creating the world was completed at the first Shabbat.

PRAYER VOCABULARY	
Come, let us sing	לְכוּ נְרַנְּנָה
With thanksgiving	בְּתוֹדָה
For God, the Eternal, is great	כִּי אֵל גָּדוֹל יְיָ

At the beginning of the Friday evening service, Shabbat is greeted with beautiful hymns. The most famous is Lecha Dodi, which pictures Shabbat as a bride coming to meet her beloved Jewish people. It was written about 450 years ago by the poet Rabbi Solomon Halevi Alkabetz, and the first letters of each verse form an acrostic of his name.

(Find the acrostic in your prayerbook.)

Come beloved, to meet the bride.   לְכָה דּוֹדִי לִקְרַאת כַּלָּה.

Beloved, come to greet Shabbat.   פְּנֵי שַׁבָּת נְקַבְּלָה.

COME BELOVED, TO MEET THE BRIDE   לְכָה דּוֹדִי לִקְרַאת כַּלָּה

The hymn Lecha Dodi refers to Shabbat as a bride and as a queen. Referring to Shabbat in this way is an ancient tradition. The Talmud tells us that some of the ancient rabbis used to dress in festive clothes in honor of Shabbat, and when Shabbat began they would sing songs which referred to Shabbat as a queen and a bride.

Many Biblical phrases are used in the text of this hymn. It has long been a very popular part of the Friday evening service, as shown by the fact that there are over one hundred melodies to which the words may be sung.

PRAYER VOCABULARY

Come beloved	לְכָה דּוֹדִי
To meet the bride	לִקְרַאת כַּלָּה
Let us greet	נְקַבְּלָה

Although it is permissible to pray most of the prayers of the service by oneself, Jews usually pray in a congregation together with other Jews. Judaism is a community religion, and prayer is a community experience. Praying with our fellow Jews makes our own prayers more meaningful. By sharing our deepest joys and sorrows, fears and hopes, we draw comfort and strength from each other.

Some prayers, such as the Barchu and Kaddish, must be said in the presence of a congregation. In order to have a congregation it is necessary to have a minyan—ten or more Jews over the age of bar mitzvah who have gathered for the purpose of prayer. Some congregations have retained the tradition to count only men in a minyan, while some temples also count women. A congregation does not have to meet in a beautiful synagogue or in a special building of any kind. In Judaism it is the people not the place that makes a congregation. As long as a minyan is present, congregational worship can take place in a tent or a rented hall or even out of doors around a campfire.

The importance of congregational prayer in Judaism is shown by the Talmudic interpretation of the Biblical statement, "May my prayers to You be in an acceptable time" (Psalms 69:14). The Talmud asks, "What is an acceptable time?" and answers, "When the congregation prays." In other words, the Talmudic rabbis felt that prayers were most acceptable to God when they emanated from an assembly of Jews praying together.

PRAYER VOCABULARY	
A quorum (ten people)	מִנְיָן
Synagogue	בֵּית כְּנֶסֶת
Congregation	קָהָל
Prayers	תְּפִלּוֹת

Services in the synagogue are made more beautiful and meaningful because the prayers are sung or are accompanied by music. Some of the lovely melodies that are used go back to ancient days, but many were written in our own time by talented musicians who wished to help beautify the service. Sometimes prayers are sung by a cantor (חַזָן) or a choir. Other times they are sung by the entire congregation.

We learn from the Bible that music was an important part of the Jewish service even in the days of the Bet Hamikdash. The shofar, one of the earliest musical instruments used for worship, is still used in our High Holy Day services. Other musical instruments were also played as part of the Temple service. Among these were the chalil, a kind of flute, the gitit, a stringed instrument, and the tof, a percussion instrument.

It is believed that before there were prayers, people expressed their feelings for God by singing chants that had no words. Later, written prayers were set to these chants. The Torah portion is still chanted to an ancient melody.

Many synagogues have a cantor (chazan) to lead the singing. At one time only a man could be a chazan, but now almost as many women as men are becoming cantors. The chazan is specially trained to sing the music of the service. Many beautiful melodies are sung, and usually each congregation has its own favorites. But whatever music is used for the service, it unquestionably does a great deal to make the service more beautiful and to help the worshippers express their innermost feelings.

PRAYER VOCABULARY

Choir	מַקְהֵלָה
Cantor	חַזָן
Shofar	שׁוֹפָר
Flute	חָלִיל
Stringed instrument	גִתִּית
Percussion instrument	תּוֹף

The formal service begins with the Call to Prayer, the Barchu. In ancient times this prayer marked the beginning of the public service, and it can be traced back to the days of the Bet Hamikdash (Temple).

Praise God to whom praise is due.	בָּרְכוּ אֶת־יְיָ הַמְבֹרָךְ.
Praise God to whom praise is due forever and ever.	בָּרוּךְ יְיָ הַמְבֹרָךְ לְעוֹלָם וָעֶד.

PRAISE GOD TO WHOM PRAISE IS DUE   בָּרְכוּ אֶת־יְיָ הַמְבֹרָךְ

The Barchu is the official beginning of the public prayer service. Since public prayer requires a minyan, or quorum, of ten worshippers, this prayer is not said unless there are at least ten worshippers present at the service.

PRAYER VOCABULARY

Praise	בָּרְכוּ
To whom praise is due	הַמְבֹרָךְ
Forever and ever	לְעוֹלָם וָעֶד

שְׁמַע וּבִרְכוֹתֶיהָ

The Shema is one of the most important prayers in the Siddur. It is taken from the Torah and declares our belief that there is only one God. It is the central theme of every worship service. It is such an important prayer that many children are taught to say it as a bedtime prayer, and many Jews who are facing death recite it to express their faith in God regardless of what happens to them.

Although we take our belief in one God for granted, people did not always recognize that there was one God who was the divine Creator and ruler of all people. That is a lesson that the Jews taught the world. Even today, there are religions that do not recognize the oneness of God. That is why it is so important to say the Shema. It reminds us that the oneness of God is the basic belief of our religion.

PRAYER VOCABULARY

Shema	שְׁמַע
Five Books of Moses, Torah	חֻמָשׁ
Prayerbook	סִדּוּר
Prayer	תְּפִלָה

The next two prayers are said before the Shema. In the first, we thank God for creating day and night, and the seasons of the year. In the second we thank God for showing love for us by giving us the Torah with its laws and mitzvot to guide us.

Blessed is the Eternal our God, ruler of the world,

בָּרוּךְ אַתָּה יְיָ אֱלֹהֵינוּ מֶלֶךְ הָעוֹלָם,

    whose word brings on the evening twilight,

אֲשֶׁר בִּדְבָרוֹ מַעֲרִיב עֲרָבִים,

    and whose wisdom opens the gates of the heavens

בְּחָכְמָה פּוֹתֵחַ שְׁעָרִים,

    God's understanding makes time pass

וּבִתְבוּנָה מְשַׁנֶּה עִתִּים,

    and the seasons change.

וּמַחֲלִיף אֶת־הַזְּמַנִּים,

    God controls the stars as they

וּמְסַדֵּר אֶת־הַכּוֹכָבִים בְּמִשְׁמְרוֹתֵיהֶם

        move across the sky.

בָּרָקִיעַ, כִּרְצוֹנוֹ.

God is the creator of day and night,

בּוֹרֵא יוֹם וָלָיְלָה,

    who makes light follow darkness

גּוֹלֵל אוֹר מִפְּנֵי־חֹשֶׁךְ

    and darkness follow light,

וְחֹשֶׁךְ מִפְּנֵי־אוֹר,

    who causes day to pass and night to come

וּמַעֲבִיר יוֹם וּמֵבִיא לָיְלָה,

    and sets them apart.

וּמַבְדִּיל בֵּין יוֹם וּבֵין לָיְלָה,

The Eternal, God of all people, is Your name.

יְיָ צְבָאוֹת שְׁמוֹ.

WHOSE WORD BRINGS THE TWILIGHT   אֲשֶׁר בִּדְבָרוֹ מַעֲרִיב עֲרָבִים

    This prayer expresses the sense of awe that we all feel when we think about the wonders of nature. Night follows day; the sun rises and sets; the planets and stars are in their expected places; and the seasons change in a regular pattern.

    One of the important ideas of this prayer is that God's word—that is, God's command—causes changes in nature. Judaism teaches not only that the world was created at the beginning of time but also that it is created anew each day in a regular rotation and pattern—all by God's command.

Our God is a living God אֵל חַי וְקַיָּם,

who will rule over us forever. תָּמִיד יִמְלוֹךְ עָלֵינוּ לְעוֹלָם וָעֶד.

Blessed is the Eternal, בָּרוּךְ אַתָּה יְיָ,
who brings the evening twilight. הַמַּעֲרִיב עֲרָבִים.

PRAYER VOCABULARY

Shema	שְׁמַע
Who brings the evening twilight	הַמַּעֲרִיב עֲרָבִים
God who creates day and night	בּוֹרֵא יוֹם וָלָיְלָה
Stars	כּוֹכָבִים
Sky	רָקִיעַ
Day	יוֹם
Night	לַיְלָה
Darkness	חֹשֶׁךְ
Light	אוֹר
Our God is a living God	אֵל חַי וְקַיָּם

Just as parents show their love for their children by teaching them how to behave properly, so too God shows love for the Jewish people by guiding them in the ways of Torah and mitzvot.

O God, You have loved the Jewish people with an enduring love.

אַהֲבַת עוֹלָם בֵּית יִשְׂרָאֵל עַמְּךָ אָהָבְתָּ.

You have taught us the Torah, the mitzvot,

תּוֹרָה וּמִצְוֹת,

and the rules of proper conduct.

חֻקִּים וּמִשְׁפָּטִים אוֹתָנוּ לִמַּדְתָּ.

Therefore, O Eternal our God,

עַל־כֵּן יְיָ אֱלֹהֵינוּ,

when we go to bed and when we wake up,

בְּשָׁכְבֵּנוּ וּבְקוּמֵנוּ

we study Your rules

נָשִׂיחַ בְּחֻקֶּיךָ,

And rejoice in the words of Your Torah and Your mitzvot forever.

וְנִשְׂמַח בְּדִבְרֵי תוֹרָתֶךָ וּבְמִצְוֹתֶיךָ
לְעוֹלָם וָעֶד.

O GOD, YOU HAVE LOVED THE JEWISH PEOPLE WITH AN ENDURING LOVE

אַהֲבַת עוֹלָם בֵּית יִשְׂרָאֵל עַמְּךָ אָהָבְתָּ

During many periods of history, the Jews were persecuted by those around them. Often their material possessions were taken away from them. But God's love and the precious ideas of the Torah could never be taken away.

The phrase אַהֲבַת עוֹלָם ("enduring love") was used by the prophet Jeremiah (31:3) to describe God's love for the Jewish people. Jeremiah was one of the prophets who tried to comfort the Jewish people after the Babylonian conquest in 586 B.C.E. The prophet believed that God would restore the Jewish people to their land as an expression of the "enduring love" referred to in this prayer.

WE REJOICE IN THE WORDS OF YOUR TORAH   וְנִשְׂמַח בְּדִבְרֵי תוֹרָתֶךָ

אַהֲבַת עוֹלָם tells of God's love for the Jewish people. One of the ways we can show our love for God is by acting kindly and lovingly to each other. Think of the people you know. Whom can you treat more kindly? Whom can you get to know better? What can you do to make things easier for someone you love?

Show your love of God by doing an act of kindness to an old friend or by making a new friend.

Because they are our life,   כִּי הֵם חַיֵּינוּ

  and give meaning to our days.   וְאֹרֶךְ יָמֵינוּ,

  We study them day and night.   וּבָהֶם נֶהְגֶּה יוֹמָם וָלָיְלָה.

Do not ever turn Your love from us.   וְאַהֲבָתְךָ אַל־תָּסִיר מִמֶּנּוּ לְעוֹלָמִים.

Blessed is the Eternal   בָּרוּךְ אַתָּה יְיָ,

  who loves the Jewish people.   אוֹהֵב עַמּוֹ יִשְׂרָאֵל.

PRAYER VOCABULARY	
Enduring love	אַהֲבַת עוֹלָם
We will rejoice	וְנִשְׂמַח
In the words of Your Torah	בְּדִבְרֵי תוֹרָתֶךָ
We study them day and night	וּבָהֶם נֶהְגֶּה יוֹמָם וָדָיְלָה
The Jewish people	עַמּוֹ יִשְׂרָאֵל

The Shema is a central prayer of our faith. In it we declare our belief in one God who is the God of all people.

Hear, O Israel, the Eternal is our God, the Eternal is one.

שְׁמַע יִשְׂרָאֵל, יְיָ אֱלֹהֵינוּ יְיָ אֶחָד!

Praised is the name of God,

בָּרוּךְ שֵׁם כְּבוֹד מַלְכוּתוֹ לְעוֹלָם וָעֶד.

whose glorious kingdom is forever.

HEAR, O ISRAEL, THE ETERNAL IS OUR GOD, THE ETERNAL IS ONE

שְׁמַע יִשְׂרָאֵל יְיָ אֱלֹהֵינוּ יְיָ אֶחָד

When all the other nations of the world still worshipped idols, the Jewish people worshipped one God. The many gods of the pagan religions cared nothing about morality and ethical values. The Jews were the first people to recognize not only that one God ruled over the entire universe but that God demanded justice and morality. This kind of religious belief is called *ethical monotheism*.

The words of the Shema express the belief of Jews everywhere that there is just one God. So important is this belief that Jews who are dying utter these words as an expression of their faith. Many Jewish martyrs have died with the Shema on their lips.

The word Israel (יִשְׂרָאֵל) refers to the entire Jewish people—those who live in the Land of Israel as well as those who live in other countries. The Jews are called the Children of Israel after our forefather Jacob, whose name was changed to Israel after he wrestled with the angel. You will find this story in the Bible (Genesis 32).

PRAYER VOCABULARY

Hear, O Israel	שְׁמַע יִשְׂרָאֵל
The Eternal is one	יְיָ אֶחָד
Whose glorious kingdom is forever	מַלְכוּתוֹ לְעוֹלָם וָעֶד

In the first paragraph of the Shema we express our love for God, promising to remember God's teachings at all times and to follow God's law.

Love the Eternal, your God	וְאָהַבְתָּ אֵת יְיָ אֱלֹהֶיךָ
with all your heart, with all your soul,	בְּכָל־לְבָבְךָ וּבְכָל־נַפְשְׁךָ
and with all your might.	וּבְכָל־מְאֹדֶךָ.
The things I command you to do should be in your heart.	וְהָיוּ הַדְּבָרִים הָאֵלֶּה אֲשֶׁר אָנֹכִי מְצַוְּךָ הַיּוֹם, עַל־לְבָבֶךָ.
Teach them carefully to your children.	וְשִׁנַּנְתָּם לְבָנֶיךָ,
Speak about them when you sit in your homes	וְדִבַּרְתָּ בָּם בְּשִׁבְתְּךָ בְּבֵיתֶךָ
and when you go on a journey;	וּבְלֶכְתְּךָ בַדֶּרֶךְ,
when you lie down and when you awake.	וּבְשָׁכְבְּךָ וּבְקוּמֶךָ.
Tie them as a sign upon your hand, and	וּקְשַׁרְתָּם לְאוֹת עַל־יָדֶךָ,
let them be as a symbol	וְהָיוּ לְטֹטָפֹת
between your eyes.	בֵּין עֵינֶיךָ.
Write them upon the doorposts of your home	וּכְתַבְתָּם עַל־מְזֻזוֹת בֵּיתֶךָ
and inside your gates.	וּבִשְׁעָרֶיךָ.

LOVE THE ETERNAL YOUR GOD WITH ALL YOUR HEART וְאָהַבְתָּ אֵת יְיָ אֱלֹהֶיךָ בְּכָל־לְבָבְךָ

The words of the Veahavta come from the Torah (Deuteronomy 6:5-9). They tell us that we should love God and obey God's laws. They also tell us that each generation must teach the laws to the next generation. The stress on teaching the values of our religion has always been very important in Judaism. Jews have always emphasized learning, both religious and secular. Even in periods when most people were illiterate and ignorant, the Jews were always educated. In our own time most Jews attach great importance to learning and knowledge.

TIE THEM AS A SIGN UPON YOUR HAND

וּקְשַׁרְתָּם לְאוֹת עַל־יָדֶךָ

"Make them as a sign upon your hand and let them be a symbol between your eyes" refers to the tefillin, or phylacteries, put on each morning for prayer by many traditional Jewish men. A set of tefillin consists of two small leather boxes with long leather straps attached. Inside the boxes are small parchments with verses from the Bible. The boxes are attached to the arm and head by means of the straps.

WRITE THEM UPON THE DOORPOSTS OF YOUR HOME

וּכְתַבְתָּם עַל־מְזֻזֹות בֵּיתֶךָ

This verse refers to the mezuzah, a small decorative case containing a parchment on which is written the first two paragraph of the Shema. The mezuzah is placed on the doorposts of Jewish homes. Some Jews, as they are leaving or entering the house, touch their fingers to the mezuzah and then kiss their fingers to show their love for the words written inside.

PRAYER VOCABULARY

Love the Eternal	וְאָהַבְתָּ אֵת יְיָ
Teach them carefully to your children	וְשִׁנַּנְתָּם לְבָנֶיךָ
Speak about them	וְדִבַּרְתָּ בָּם
Upon the doorposts of your home	עַל־מְזֻזֹות בֵּיתֶךָ
Inside your gates	וּבִשְׁעָרֶיךָ

This is the second paragraph of the Shema which tells of the rewards for those who listen to God's words.

If you listen to my commandments	וְהָיָה אִם־שָׁמֹעַ תִּשְׁמְעוּ אֶל־מִצְוֺתַי
which I command you today	אֲשֶׁר אָנֹכִי מְצַוֶּה אֶתְכֶם הַיּוֹם
to love the Eternal, your God,	לְאַהֲבָה אֶת־יְיָ אֱלֹהֵיכֶם
and to serve God with all your heart	וּלְעָבְדוֹ בְּכָל־לְבַבְכֶם
and with all your soul,	וּבְכָל־נַפְשְׁכֶם:
Then will I give the rain for your land in its proper season,	וְנָתַתִּי מְטַר־אַרְצְכֶם בְּעִתּוֹ
the autumn rain and the spring rain,	יוֹרֶה וּמַלְקוֹשׁ
and you will gather your grain,	וְאָסַפְתָּ דְגָנֶךָ
your wine, and your oil.	וְתִירֹשְׁךָ וְיִצְהָרֶךָ:
And I will also give grass in your fields for your livestock.	וְנָתַתִּי עֵשֶׂב בְּשָׂדְךָ לִבְהֶמְתֶּךָ
So shall you eat and be satisfied.	וְאָכַלְתָּ וְשָׂבָעְתָּ:
However, be careful, lest your heart be fooled	הִשָּׁמְרוּ לָכֶם פֶּן־יִפְתֶּה לְבַבְכֶם
and you turn away from the Almighty	וְסַרְתֶּם
to serve other gods	וַעֲבַדְתֶּם אֱלֹהִים אֲחֵרִים
and worship them.	וְהִשְׁתַּחֲוִיתֶם לָהֶם:

For then the Almighty's anger will rise against you.

וְחָרָה אַף־יְיָ בָּכֶם

God will shut the heavens so that they shall not provide rain,

וְעָצַר אֶת־הַשָּׁמַיִם וְלֹא־יִהְיֶה מָטָר

and the earth will not give forth its produce.

וְהָאֲדָמָה לֹא תִתֵּן אֶת־יְבוּלָהּ

Then you shall quickly vanish from off the good land

וַאֲבַדְתֶּם מְהֵרָה מֵעַל הָאָרֶץ הַטֹּבָה

which God gives you.

אֲשֶׁר יְיָ נֹתֵן לָכֶם:

Therefore, you should place these, my words,

וְשַׂמְתֶּם אֶת־דְּבָרַי אֵלֶּה

upon your heart and your soul.

עַל־לְבַבְכֶם וְעַל־נַפְשְׁכֶם

Tie them as a sign upon your hands,

וּקְשַׁרְתֶּם אֹתָם לְאוֹת עַל־יֶדְכֶם

and they shall be a symbol between your eyes.

וְהָיוּ לְטוֹטָפֹת בֵּין עֵינֵיכֶם:

Teach them to your children

וְלִמַּדְתֶּם אֹתָם אֶת־בְּנֵיכֶם

speaking of them

לְדַבֵּר בָּם

when you are at home,

בְּשִׁבְתְּךָ בְּבֵיתֶךָ

and when you go on a journey,

וּבְלֶכְתְּךָ בַדֶּרֶךְ

when you go to bed, and when you wake up.

וּבְשָׁכְבְּךָ וּבְקוּמֶךָ:

And write them upon the doorposts of your house and within your gates.

וּכְתַבְתָּם עַל־מְזוּזוֹת בֵּיתֶךָ וּבִשְׁעָרֶיךָ:

WHEN YOU GO TO BED AND WHEN YOU WAKE UP   וּבְשָׁכְבְּךָ וּבְקוּמֶךָ

Here we are commanded to remember God's words, speaking of them even when we lie down at night and when we wake up in the morning. This is the basis for reciting the Shema twice a day, morning and evening.

So that your days and the days of your children will be many

לְמַעַן יִרְבּוּ יְמֵיכֶם וִימֵי בְנֵיכֶם

upon this land

עַל הָאֲדָמָה

which the Eternal promised to your ancestors

אֲשֶׁר נִשְׁבַּע יְיָ לַאֲבֹתֵיכֶם

to give to them

לָתֵת לָהֶם

so long as the heavens are above the earth.

כִּימֵי הַשָּׁמַיִם עַל־הָאָרֶץ:

48

This is the third paragraph of the Shema which explains the commandment of Tsitsit.

Then God spoke to Moses:	וַיֹּאמֶר יְיָ אֶל־מֹשֶׁה לֵּאמֹר:
Speak to the children of Israel.	דַּבֵּר אֶל־בְּנֵי יִשְׂרָאֵל
Tell them that they shall put fringes	וְאָמַרְתָּ אֲלֵהֶם וְעָשׂוּ לָהֶם צִיצִת
on the corners of their clothes	עַל־כַּנְפֵי בִגְדֵיהֶם
for all generations.	לְדֹרֹתָם
They shall place on the fringe of the corner	וְנָתְנוּ עַל־צִיצִת הַכָּנָף
a blue thread.	פְּתִיל תְּכֵלֶת:
And it shall be for you a fringe,	וְהָיָה לָכֶם לְצִיצִת
so that you shall see it	וּרְאִיתֶם אֹתוֹ
and remember all the commandments of the Eternal One	וּזְכַרְתֶּם אֶת־כָּל־מִצְוֹת יְיָ
and do them.	וַעֲשִׂיתֶם אֹתָם

וְהָיָה לָכֶם לְצִיצִת וּרְאִיתֶם אֹתוֹ

AND IT SHALL BE TO YOU FOR A FRINGE SO THAT YOU SHALL SEE IT

Our rabbis determined from this biblical verse that the commandment of wearing Tsitsit with fringes applies only when the fringes can be seen, that is, in the daytime. That is why the Tallit is worn for the daytime services but not at the evening service.

49

So that you shall not stray after the desires of	וְלֹא תָתּוּרוּ אַחֲרֵי
your heart and your eyes	לְבַבְכֶם וְאַחֲרֵי עֵינֵיכֶם
for which you long.	אֲשֶׁר־אַתֶּם זֹנִים אַחֲרֵיהֶם:
Thus you will remember	לְמַעַן תִּזְכְּרוּ
and perform all My commandments	וַעֲשִׂיתֶם אֶת־כָּל־מִצְוֺתָי
so that you will be holy to your God.	וִהְיִיתֶם קְדֹשִׁים לֵאלֹהֵיכֶם:
I am the Eternal One, Your God,	אֲנִי יְיָ אֱלֹהֵיכֶם
Who brought you out	אֲשֶׁר הוֹצֵאתִי אֶתְכֶם
of the Land of Egypt	מֵאֶרֶץ מִצְרַיִם
to be Your God.	לִהְיוֹת לָכֶם לֵאלֹהִים
I am the Eternal One, Your God.	אֲנִי יְיָ אֱלֹהֵיכֶם: אֱמֶת:

PRAYER VOCABULARY

Tsitsit, fringes	צִיצָת
So that you shall see it	וּרְאִיתֶם אֹתוֹ
And remember all the commandments of the Eternal One	וּזְכַרְתֶּם אֶת־כָּל־מִצְוֺת יְיָ
From the Land of Egypt	מֵאֶרֶץ מִצְרַיִם
Thus you will remember	לְמַעַן תִּזְכְּרוּ
Thus will you become holy	וִהְיִיתֶם קְדוֹשִׁים
Phylacteries	תְּפִילִין
Mezuzah	מְזוּזָה

מִי־כָמְכָה

The prayer Mee Chamocha follows the Shema and Veahavta. This prayer is from the Bible. It is the hymn of praise that Moses sang to God after he led the Israelites across the Red Sea. The exodus from Egypt was one of the most important events in Jewish history. This prayer ties us to our past and helps us to remember that God has watched over the Jewish people in all lands and all ages.

Who is like You among the mighty, O Eternal?	מִי־כָמְכָה בָּאֵלִים יְיָ?
Who is like You, great in holiness?	מִי כָּמְכָה נֶאְדָּר בַּקֹּדֶשׁ?
Impressive and splendid, doing wonders.	נוֹרָא תְהִלֹּת עֹשֵׂה פֶלֶא.
The Eternal shall rule forever and ever.	יְיָ יִמְלֹךְ לְעֹלָם וָעֶד:

WHO IS LIKE YOU AMONG THE MIGHTY, O ETERNAL? מִי־כָמְכָה בָּאֵלִים יְיָ

The first letters of the first four words of this prayer (מַכַּבִּי) spell Maccabee in Hebrew. It is said that Judah Maccabee took his name from this prayer because the words were symbolic of his devotion and loyalty to God.

PRAYER VOCABULARY

Who is like You among the mighty, O Eternal?	מִי כָמְכָה בָּאֵלִים יְיָ
Doing wonders	עֹשֵׂה פֶלֶא

A prayer for the deliverance of Israel.

It has been said,"The Eternal delivered Jacob from a force mightier than he."

וְנֶאֱמַר, כִּי־פָדָה יְיָ אֶת־יַעֲקֹב,
וּגְאָלוֹ מִיַּד חָזָק מִמֶּנּוּ.

Blessed is the Eternal who delivered Israel.

בָּרוּךְ אַתָּה יְיָ,
גָּאַל יִשְׂרָאֵל.

PRAYER VOCABULARY

It has been said	וְנֶאֱמַר
From a force mightier than he	מִיַּד חָזָק מִמֶּנּוּ
Who delivered Israel	גָּאַל יִשְׂרָאֵל

**Hashkivenu is a beautiful prayer that asks God to
protect us with peace and safeguard us from harm.**

O Eternal, our God, may we go to bed in peace	הַשְׁכִּיבֵנוּ יְיָ אֱלֹהֵינוּ לְשָׁלוֹם,
and awake to renewed life.	וְהַעֲמִידֵנוּ מַלְכֵּנוּ לְחַיִּים.
Spread over us a roof of peace.	וּפְרוֹשׂ עָלֵינוּ סֻכַּת שְׁלוֹמֶךָ,
Guide us with good advice and be	וְתַקְּנֵנוּ בְּעֵצָה טוֹבָה מִלְּפָנֶיךָ,
our helper for the sake of Your name.	וְהוֹשִׁיעֵנוּ לְמַעַן שְׁמֶךָ.
Shield us from hatred and illness.	וְהָגֵן בַּעֲדֵנוּ, וְהָסֵר מֵעָלֵינוּ אוֹיֵב,
Protect us from war, famine, and suffering.	דֶּבֶר וְחֶרֶב, וְרָעָב, וְיָגוֹן,
and remove our enemies from before and from behind us,	וְהָסֵר שָׂטָן מִלְּפָנֵינוּ וּמֵאַחֲרֵינוּ,
Shelter us in the shadow of Your wings,	וּבְצֵל כְּנָפֶיךָ תַּסְתִּירֵנוּ,
because You are a protective God.	כִּי אֵל שׁוֹמְרֵנוּ וּמַצִּילֵנוּ אָתָּה,
and a masterful ruler.	כִּי אֵל מֶלֶךְ חַנּוּן וְרַחוּם אָתָּה.
Watch over us in our goings and our comings	וּשְׁמֹר צֵאתֵנוּ וּבוֹאֵנוּ,
so that we may have life and peace,	לְחַיִּים וּלְשָׁלוֹם,
now and always.	מֵעַתָּה וְעַד עוֹלָם.
Spread over us a roof of peace.	וּפְרֹשׂ עָלֵינוּ סֻכַּת שְׁלוֹמֶךָ.
Blessed is the Eternal,	בָּרוּךְ אַתָּה יְיָ,
who protects us,	הַפּוֹרֵשׂ סֻכַּת שָׁלוֹם עָלֵינוּ
the people of Israel,	וְעַל כָּל עַמּוֹ יִשְׂרָאֵל,
and Jerusalem with peace.	וְעַל יְרוּשָׁלָיִם.

ETERNAL, OUR GOD, MAY WE GO TO BED IN PEACE הַשְׁכִּיבֵנוּ יְיָ אֱלֹהֵינוּ לְשָׁלוֹם

Many people (adults as well as children) find the night frightening. They feel safer and more secure during the day. In this prayer we ask to be protected as we sleep. But our prayers are not for ourselves alone. We also ask that the entire people of Israel be protected with God's peace.

May we go to bed	הַשְׁכִּיבֵנוּ
And spread over us	וּפְרֹשׂ עָלֵינוּ
A roof of peace	סֻכַּת שְׁלוֹמֶךָ
Watch over us in our goings	וּשְׁמוֹר צֵאתֵנוּ

Hashkivenu is followed by the singing of the beautiful Shabbat hymn Veshamru.

The people of Israel shall keep Shabbat	וְשָׁמְרוּ בְנֵי־יִשְׂרָאֵל אֶת־הַשַּׁבָּת,
and observe it in every generation as a covenant for all time.	לַעֲשׂוֹת אֶת הַשַּׁבָּת לְדֹרֹתָם, בְּרִית עוֹלָם.
Between Me and the people of Israel,	בֵּינִי וּבֵין בְּנֵי־יִשְׂרָאֵל
it is a sign forever,	אוֹת הִיא לְעוֹלָם,
for in six days God created heaven and earth,	כִּי־שֵׁשֶׁת יָמִים עָשָׂה יְיָ אֶת־הַשָּׁמַיִם וְאֶת־הָאָרֶץ,
and on the seventh day God rested from this work.	וּבַיּוֹם הַשְּׁבִיעִי שָׁבַת וַיִּנָּפַשׁ.

THE PEOPLE OF ISRAEL SHALL KEEP SHABBAT   וְשָׁמְרוּ בְנֵי־יִשְׂרָאֵל אֶת־הַשַּׁבָּת

Although Shabbat comes every week, it is considered the most sacred holiday, second only to Yom Kippur. It has been cherished by the Jews through the ages as a day of rest and tranquility.

FOR IN SIX DAYS GOD CREATED HEAVEN AND EARTH

כִּי־שֵׁשֶׁת יָמִים עָשָׂה יְיָ   אֶת־הַשָּׁמַיִם וְאֶת־הָאָרֶץ

The Biblical story of creation in Genesis tells of the creation of the world by God in six days. On the seventh day, God rested from the work of creation. In commemoration, we too rest on the seventh day of the week—Shabbat.

PRAYER VOCABULARY

The children of Israel shall keep the Sabbath	וְשָׁמְרוּ בְנֵי־יִשְׂרָאֵל אֶת־הַשַּׁבָּת
As a covenant for all time	בְּרִית עוֹלָם
It is a sign forever	אוֹת הִיא לְעֹלָם
For in six days	כִּי־שֵׁשֶׁת יָמִים
God rested from His work	שָׁבַת וַיִּנָּפַשׁ

LEARNING MORE ABOUT: THE LANGUAGE OF PRAYER

Most of the prayers in our prayerbook are in Hebrew. Long ago Hebrew was the everyday language of the Jews in Israel. Today it is again the everyday language of the Jews who live in Israel. But for many, many years in between, Hebrew was not the language of ordinary conversation. It was considered the holy language (lashon hakodesh) because it is the language in which the Bible was written.

When many of the prayers in our Siddur were written, the Jews spoke Aramaic. The Aramaic language is similar to Hebrew. Although the poets spoke Aramaic as an everyday language, they did not generally use it when writing prayers.

Instead they used Hebrew, the holy language. Just a few of our prayers were written in Aramaic. The Kaddish is one of them. Later in this book, when you learn to read the Kaddish, you will be able to compare some of the differences between Hebrew and Aramaic.

In addition to Hebrew, Jews often pray in the language of their country. French Jews say prayers in French, Italian Jews say prayers in Italian, and American Jews say prayers in English. But they all say *most* of their prayers in Hebrew. So if you go to a service in any country of the world, you will be able to join in the Hebrew prayers.

PRAYER VOCABULARY

Hebrew	עִבְרִית
Prayerbook	סִדוּר
Holy language	לָשׁוֹן (הַ)קוֹדֶשׁ
Prayer	תְּפִלָּה

III. THE AMIDAH

The Amidah is one of the most important parts of the worship service. Along with the Shema, the Kaddish, and the Alenu, it is included in every prayer service, whether Shabbat, holiday, or weekday.

The Amidah is divided into three groups of blessings. The blessings in the first group praise God and describe God's love for the people of Israel. The blessings in the second group are prayers of petition. The blessings in the third group are prayers of thanksgiving to God for all the good things in our lives.

While the basic Amidah is recited three times daily, its content varies depending on the nature of the day. For example, on Shabbat only the blessings that praise God and the blessings that thank God are recited. The middle portion of the Amidah, the prayers of petition, in which we ask God for specific things such as wisdom, understanding, good health, and a grateful disposition, are recited only on weekdays. The rabbis who compiled the Siddur did not think it right to ask God for specific things on Shabbat. They felt it was not in the spirit of Shabbat for us to ask for things for ourselves. Instead of the prayers of petition, special Shabbat prayers are added to the Amidah, such as Veshamru and Yismechu, which emphasize the joy and holiness of Shabbat. In addition, we make mention of the sacrifices that were brought in the *Bet Hamikdash* on Shabbat. On holidays we add prayers of joy, reminders of the holiday sacrifices, and on *Rosh Hashanah* and *Yom Kippur*, prayers asking for forgiveness.

The Amidah is known by three names. Shemoneh Esrey, meaning "eighteen," came into use because the prayer was originally made up of eighteen separate blessings, and it is still used even though the prayer now has nineteen blessings. The word Amidah means "standing," and the name of the prayer is derived from the practice of standing when it is recited. This prayer has also simply been called Hatefillah, the prayer, because it is the core of the service.

Shemoneh Esrey (18)	שְׁמוֹנֶה עֶשְׂרֵה
Amidah (standing)	עֲמִידָה

In the first paragraph of the Amidah, we direct our prayers to the same God who provided comfort for our ancestors. Our religion is our link to the past history of our people.

Blessed is the Eternal, Our God and
God of our ancestors.

בָּרוּךְ אַתָּה יְיָ, אֱלֹהֵינוּ וֵאלֹהֵי אֲבוֹתֵינוּ.

The God of Abraham, Isaac, and Jacob,

אֱלֹהֵי אַבְרָהָם, אֱלֹהֵי יִצְחָק וֵאלֹהֵי יַעֲקֹב.

the great, mighty, and all-powerful

הָאֵל הַגָּדוֹל הַגִּבּוֹר וְהַנּוֹרָא,

exalted God

אֵל עֶלְיוֹן,

who in kindness and love created

גּוֹמֵל חֲסָדִים טוֹבִים,

everything, and who remembers
the good deeds of our ancestors

וְקֹנֵה הַכֹּל וְזוֹכֵר חַסְדֵי אָבוֹת,

and brings a redeemer to
their children's children

וּמֵבִיא גוֹאֵל לִבְנֵי בְנֵיהֶם

for Your name's sake with love.

לְמַעַן שְׁמוֹ בְּאַהֲבָה.

You are our ruler, helper, deliverer,
and shield.

מֶלֶךְ עוֹזֵר וּמוֹשִׁיעַ וּמָגֵן.

Blessed is the Eternal,
the shield of Abraham.

בָּרוּךְ אַתָּה יְיָ, מָגֵן אַבְרָהָם.

BLESSED IS THE ETERNAL, OUR GOD AND THE GOD OF OUR ANCESTORS. THE GOD OF ABRAHAM, ISAAC AND JACOB

בָּרוּךְ אַתָּה יְיָ, אֱלֹהֵינוּ וֵאלֹהֵי אֲבוֹתֵינוּ. אֱלֹהֵי אַבְרָהָם, אֱלֹהֵי יִצְחָק וֵאלֹהֵי יַעֲקֹב

This prayer refers to our ancestors Abraham, Isaac, and Jacob. Abraham was the first to accept the oneness of God. The Bible tells the story of Abraham's great love for God. To illustrate Abraham's devotion and loyalty to God, it relates the story of Akedat Yitzchak, the binding of Isaac. When God asked Abraham to sacrifice Isaac, his only son whom he loved very much, Abraham did not hesitate. Isaac was eventually spared, and God promised to bless Abraham and make his descendants as numerous as the stars in the sky and the sands of the beach. You and I and all the Jews of the world are the descendants of Abraham.

PRAYER VOCABULARY	
Prayer	תְּפִלָּה
And brings a redeemer	וּמֵבִיא גוֹאֵל
The shield of Abraham	מָגֵן אַבְרָהָם

The second paragraph of the Amidah, Ata Gibor (You are mighty), recognizes that God is the source of life for all humankind.

You are mighty, O God,	אַתָּה גִּבּוֹר לְעוֹלָם, אֲדֹנָי,
You call the dead to immortal life	מְחַיֵּה מֵתִים אַתָּה
For you are mighty in deliverance.	רַב לְהוֹשִׁיעַ.
You support the living with compassion	מְכַלְכֵּל חַיִּים בְּחֶסֶד,
You call the dead to life with great mercy.	מְחַיֵּה מֵתִים בְּרַחֲמִים רַבִּים:
You raise the fallen, heal the sick,	סוֹמֵךְ נוֹפְלִים וְרוֹפֵא חוֹלִים,
and free the captives.	וּמַתִּיר אֲסוּרִים,
You keep faith with those who have returned to dust.	וּמְקַיֵּם אֱמוּנָתוֹ לִישֵׁנֵי עָפָר.
Who is like You, O doer of mighty deeds,	מִי כָמוֹךָ, בַּעַל גְּבוּרוֹת,
and who resembles You?	וּמִי דוֹמֶה־לָּךְ.?
Ruler who decrees both death and life	מֶלֶךְ מֵמִית וּמְחַיֶּה,
and are the source of salvation.	וּמַצְמִיחַ יְשׁוּעָה.
You keep Your promise to return the dead to eternal life.	וְנֶאֱמָן אַתָּה לְהַחֲיוֹת מֵתִים
Blessed are You, O Eternal,	בָּרוּךְ אַתָּה יְיָ,
who calls the dead to eternal life.	מְחַיֵּה הַמֵּתִים:

PRAYER VOCABULARY

You are mighty	אַתָּה גִּבּוֹר
You call the dead to eternal life	מְחַיֵּה מֵתִים אַתָּה
Mighty in deliverance	רַב לְהוֹשִׁיעַ·
You raise the fallen	סוֹמֵךְ נוֹפְלִים
Heal the sick	וְרוֹפֵא חוֹלִים
And free the captives	וּמַתִּיר אֲסוּרִים

קַדְּשֵׁנוּ בְּמִצְוֺתֶיךָ

**The following paragraph asks God to accept in love
our observance of the Shabbat.**

Our God and God of our ancestors,	אֱלֹהֵינוּ וֵאלֹהֵי אֲבוֹתֵינוּ,
Accept our rest.	רְצֵה בִמְנוּחָתֵנוּ
Make us holy through Your commandments.	קַדְּשֵׁנוּ בְּמִצְוֺתֶיךָ,
Help us to follow Your Torah.	וְתֵן חֶלְקֵנוּ בְּתוֹרָתֶךָ,
Fulfill our needs in Your goodness,	שַׂבְּעֵנוּ מִטּוּבֶךָ,
and let us be happy with Your help.	וְשַׂמְּחֵנוּ בִּישׁוּעָתֶךָ,
Make our hearts pure that we may worship with You in truth,	וְטַהֵר לִבֵּנוּ לְעָבְדְּךָ בֶּאֱמֶת.
Eternal, our God, grant us	וְהַנְחִילֵנוּ יְיָ אֱלֹהֵינוּ
In your love	בְּאַהֲבָה וּבְרָצוֹן
Your holy Shabbat.	שַׁבַּת קָדְשֶׁךָ,
And may Israel rest on it and make Your name holy.	וְיָנוּחוּ בָהּ יִשְׂרָאֵל מְקַדְּשֵׁי שְׁמֶךָ.
Blessed is the Eternal, who makes the Shabbat holy.	בָּרוּךְ אַתָּה יְיָ, מְקַדֵּשׁ הַשַּׁבָּת.

PRAYER VOCABULARY

Make us holy through Your commandments	קַדְּשֵׁנוּ בְּמִצְוֺתֶיךָ
Make our hearts pure	וְטַהֵר לִבֵּנוּ
That we may worship You in truth	לְעָבְדְּךָ בֶּאֱמֶת
Who makes the Shabbat holy	מְקַדֵּשׁ הַשַּׁבָּת

Here we recall the first Shabbat. After the creation of the world in six days described in the Book of Genesis, God rested on the seventh day and blessed it.

You have made the seventh day holy to Your name	אַתָּה קִדַּשְׁתָּ אֶת־יוֹם הַשְּׁבִיעִי לִשְׁמֶךָ.
Marking the end of the creation of the heavens and earth,	תַּכְלִית מַעֲשֵׂה שָׁמַיִם וָאָרֶץ.
And you have blessed it above all days	וּבֵרַכְתּוֹ מִכָּל הַיָּמִים
And made it holy above all the seasons:	וְקִדַּשְׁתּוֹ מִכָּל־הַזְּמַנִּים
As it is written in Your Torah:	וְכֵן כָּתוּב בְּתוֹרָתֶךָ:
Then the heavens and the earth and all that was in them had been completed.	וַיְכֻלּוּ הַשָּׁמַיִם וְהָאָרֶץ וְכָל־צְבָאָם:
God finished on the Seventh Day	וַיְכַל אֱלֹהִים בַּיּוֹם הַשְּׁבִיעִי
The work which was done.	מְלַאכְתּוֹ אֲשֶׁר עָשָׂה
And God rested on the Seventh Day	וַיִּשְׁבֹּת בַּיּוֹם הַשְּׁבִיעִי
From doing all the work of creation.	מִכָּל־מְלַאכְתּוֹ אֲשֶׁר עָשָׂה:
And God blessed the Seventh Day	וַיְבָרֶךְ אֱלֹהִים אֶת־יוֹם הַשְּׁבִיעִי
and made it holy	וַיְקַדֵּשׁ אֹתוֹ.
Because on it God had rested from All the work of creation.	כִּי בוֹ שָׁבַת מִכָּל־מְלַאכְתּוֹ אֲשֶׁר בָּרָא אֱלֹהִים לַעֲשׂוֹת:

PRAYER VOCABULARY

You have made holy	אַתָּה קִדַּשְׁתָּ
The Seventh Day	יוֹם הַשְּׁבִיעִי
And blessed it	וּבֵרַכְתּוֹ
And they were finished	וַיְכֻלּוּ
The work which God did	מְלַאכְתּוֹ אֲשֶׁר עָשָׂה
(God) rested	שָׁבַת
(God) created	בָּרָא

A request that God hear our prayers.

O Eternal our God, favor Your people Israel	רְצֵה, יְיָ אֱלֹהֵינוּ, בְּעַמְּךָ יִשְׂרָאֵל,
and accept their prayers with love.	וּתְפִלָּתָם בְּאַהֲבָה תְקַבֵּל,
May Your people Israel's prayers always	וּתְהִי לְרָצוֹן תָּמִיד,
be acceptable to You.	עֲבֹדַת יִשְׂרָאֵל עַמֶּךָ.
Blessed is the Eternal,	בָּרוּךְ אַתָּה יְיָ,
whom alone we worship.	שֶׁאוֹתְךָ לְבַדְּךָ בְּיִרְאָה נַעֲבוֹד.

PRAYER VOCABULARY

Favor us	רְצֵה
Their prayers	תְפִלָּתָם
Accept with love	בְּאַהֲבָה תְקַבֵּל
Israel's prayers	עֲבֹדַת יִשְׂרָאֵל

The second of the concluding prayers of the Amidah expresses the hope that God will continue to love us and take care of us.

We thank you, O Eternal	מוֹדִים אֲנַחְנוּ לָךְ,
For you are our God	שָׁאַתָּה הוּא יְיָ אֱלֹהֵינוּ
and the God of our ancestors forever.	וֵאלֹהֵי אֲבוֹתֵינוּ, לְעוֹלָם וָעֶד.
You have been our rock and shield	צוּר חַיֵּינוּ, מָגֵן יִשְׁעֵנוּ אַתָּה הוּא
from generation to generation.	לְדוֹר וָדוֹר,
We thank You and praise You	נוֹדֶה לְּךָ וּנְסַפֵּר תְּהִלָּתֶךָ,
For our lives are in Your control,	עַל־חַיֵּינוּ הַמְּסוּרִים בְּיָדֶךָ,
And for our spirits which are in your charge,	וְעַל־נִשְׁמוֹתֵינוּ הַפְּקוּדוֹת לָךְ,
And for Your miracles which we experience every day,	וְעַל־נִסֶּיךָ שֶׁבְּכָל־יוֹם עִמָּנוּ,
And for Your wonders	וְעַל־נִפְלְאוֹתֶיךָ
And favors which You perform for us	וְטוֹבוֹתֶיךָ שֶׁבְּכָל עֵת,
Evening, morning, and noon.	עֶרֶב וָבֹקֶר וְצָהֳרָיִם.
O, Master of Goodness, Your mercies never end.	הַטּוֹב, כִּי־לֹא כָלוּ רַחֲמֶיךָ,
O, Merciful One, Your kindness never leaves us.	וְהַמְרַחֵם כִּי־לֹא תַמּוּ חֲסָדֶיךָ,
	מֵעוֹלָם קִוִּינוּ לָךְ.

WE THANK YOU   מוֹדִים אֲנַחְנוּ לָךְ

This is a prayer of thanksgiving. The Hebrew word תוֹדָה ("thank you") belongs in the same word family as מוֹדִים ("we thank you"). In this prayer we refer to God as a rock (צוּר) and a shield (מָגֵן).

PRAYER VOCABULARY

We thank You, O Eternal	מוֹדִים אֲנַחְנוּ לָךְ
Evening, morning and noon.	עֶרֶב וָבֹקֶר וְצָהֳרָיִם.
(They) never end	לֹא כָלוּ
Your mercies	רַחֲמֶיךָ

שָׁלוֹם רָב

A plea for peace for the Jewish people.

Grant everlasting peace to Your people Israel	שָׁלוֹם רָב עַל יִשְׂרָאֵל עַמְּךָ תָּשִׂים לְעוֹלָם,
For You are the ruler and master of peace.	כִּי אַתָּה הוּא מֶלֶךְ אָדוֹן לְכָל הַשָּׁלוֹם.
May it be good in Your sight to bless your people Israel	וְטוֹב בְּעֵינֶיךָ לְבָרֵךְ אֶת עַמְּךָ יִשְׂרָאֵל,
with Your peace at all times.	בְּכָל עֵת וּבְכָל שָׁעָה בִּשְׁלוֹמֶךָ.
Blessed is the Eternal,	בָּרוּךְ אַתָּה יְיָ,
who blesses the people Israel with peace.	הַמְבָרֵךְ אֶת עַמּוֹ יִשְׂרָאֵל בַּשָּׁלוֹם.

GRANT EVERLASTING PEACE TO YOUR PEOPLE ISRAEL

שָׁלוֹם רָב עַל יִשְׂרָאֵל עַמְּךָ תָּשִׂים לְעוֹלָם

The prayer for peace follows מוֹדִים אֲנַחְנוּ לָךְ , which is a prayer of thanksgiving. Our rabbis believed that without thanksgiving there can be no peace. Peace means not only peace between nations but also peace between the individual and God.

PRAYER VOCABULARY	
Everlasting peace	שָׁלוֹם רָב
The master of peace	אָדוֹן לְכָל הַשָּׁלוֹם
May it be good in your sight	וְטוֹב בְּעֵינֶיךָ
With your peace	בִּשְׁלוֹמֶךָ

IV. CONCLUDING PRAYERS עָלֵינוּ לְשַׁבֵּחַ

We bow our heads as we worship and praise God. We pray that one day the entire human race will recognize that there is one God who rules the world.

It is our duty to praise the Master of all
עָלֵינוּ לְשַׁבֵּחַ לַאֲדוֹן הַכֹּל, לָתֵת גְּדֻלָּה

And praise the One
who formed the world in the beginning.
לְיוֹצֵר בְּרֵאשִׁית,

The Eternal has not made us like the nations of other lands.
שֶׁלֹּא עָשָׂנוּ כְּגוֹיֵי הָאֲרָצוֹת,

We are set apart from other families of earth
וְלֹא שָׂמָנוּ כְּמִשְׁפְּחוֹת הָאֲדָמָה,

For our lot is not like theirs, and our destiny is unique.
שֶׁלֹּא שָׂם חֶלְקֵנוּ כָּהֶם וְגוֹרָלֵנוּ כְּכָל הֲמוֹנָם.

So we bow
וַאֲנַחְנוּ כֹּרְעִים,

as we worship and give thanks
וּמִשְׁתַּחֲוִים וּמוֹדִים

to the ruler of rulers,
לִפְנֵי מֶלֶךְ, מַלְכֵי הַמְּלָכִים,

the Holy One Whom we praise.
הַקָּדוֹשׁ בָּרוּךְ הוּא.

As it says in the Torah: God will rule over all the earth.
וְנֶאֱמַר וְהָיָה יְיָ לְמֶלֶךְ עַל־כָּל־הָאָרֶץ

On that day the Eternal will be One
בַּיוֹם הַהוּא, יִהְיֶה יְיָ אֶחָד,

and God's name will be One.
וּשְׁמוֹ אֶחָד.

WE BOW AS WE WORSHIP
וַאֲנַחְנוּ כֹּרְעִים, וּמִשְׁתַּחֲוִים

In the Alenu it is customary to bow during the recitation of the words וַאֲנַחְנוּ כֹּרְעִים ("We bow").

The Alenu became part of the daily service around the year 1300. It was originally part of the Rosh Hashanah service only. According to some rabbis, it was composed by Joshua when he first entered the Holy Land. Others believe that the author was Rav, a famous rabbi whose opinions are often quoted in the Talmud.

PRAYER VOCABULARY	
It is our duty to praise	עָלֵינוּ לְשַׁבֵּחַ
We bow	וַאֲנַחְנוּ כֹּרְעִים
The Holy One Whom we praise	הַקָּדוֹשׁ בָּרוּךְ הוּא
On that day	בַּיוֹם הַהוּא
The Eternal will be One	יִהְיֶה יְיָ אֶחָד

קַדִּישׁ

The Mourner's Kaddish is a prayer said in memory of loved ones who have died. But it does not mention anything about death or dying. It is a prayer of praise to God. Although we are not really sure how this prayer came to be associated with mourning, we believe that it probably happened in the following way.

In ancient times when a scholar died, other scholars honored his memory by gathering in his home to study the Torah. It was the custom in those days to end every session of Torah study by reciting the Kaddish as a way of praising God and expressing gratitude for the Torah. But this custom discriminated against those who were not considered scholars. When the people in the community saw that there was no gathering in the home of a person who had died, they knew that he had been an ignorant man. He would be looked down upon and his family would be shamed. In order not to embarrass the families of those who had not been scholars, it soon became the custom to study Torah and recite the Kaddish in every house of mourning. Usually the oldest son was given the honor of reciting the Kaddish after such a study session.

In this way the custom developed of having the son recite Kaddish for his father. Since Kaddish may be recited only in the presence of a minyan, the custom developed of reciting Kaddish in the synagogue in the presence of the congregation. In our time Kaddish is recited by the immediate family for parents, husband or wife, sister or brother, or children who have died.

Unlike most of the prayers in the Siddur, the Kaddish is in Aramaic rather than Hebrew. Aramaic was the everyday language of the Jews when the prayer was written. Aramaic is written in Hebrew letters. Some of the words are the same as Hebrew words and others are very similar. If you know the root letters of a Hebrew word family, you can sometimes figure out the general meaning of some of the Aramaic words. See if you can find words in the Kaddish that are in the following families:

King	מֶלֶךְ
Big	גָּדוֹל
Holy	קָדוֹשׁ
Blessed	בָּרוּךְ
Peace	שָׁלוֹם

PRAYER VOCABULARY

Kaddish	קַדִּישׁ
Scholar	תַּלְמִיד חָכָם
Congregation	קָהָל
Aramaic	אֲרַמִית

Those in the congregation who are mourning the loss of a close relative say this prayer of praise to God in remembrance of their loved one. The entire congregation responds to the Kaddish as a way of showing their compassion and sympathy for the mourners.

May God's name be made great and holy	יִתְגַּדַּל וְיִתְקַדַּשׁ שְׁמֵהּ רַבָּא
throughout the world which God created.	בְּעָלְמָא דִּי־בְרָא כִרְעוּתֵהּ.
May the divine kingdom of the Almighty	וְיַמְלִיךְ מַלְכוּתֵהּ
be established in our lifetime	בְּחַיֵּיכוֹן וּבְיוֹמֵיכוֹן
And in the life of all the House of Israel	וּבְחַיֵּי דְכָל־בֵּית יִשְׂרָאֵל,
in the near future.	בַּעֲגָלָא וּבִזְמַן קָרִיב,
Let us all say Amen.	וְאִמְרוּ אָמֵן.

The Congregation responds:

May God's great name be blessed	יְהֵא שְׁמֵהּ רַבָּא מְבָרַךְ,
forever and ever.	לְעָלַם וּלְעָלְמֵי עָלְמַיָּא.
May God's name be blessed and praised, glorified and worshipped, adored and exalted.	יִתְבָּרַךְ וְיִשְׁתַּבַּח, וְיִתְפָּאַר וְיִתְרוֹמַם, וְיִתְנַשֵּׂא, וְיִתְהַדָּר וְיִתְעַלֶּה וְיִתְהַלָּל שְׁמֵהּ דְּקוּדְשָׁא.
Blessed is the Eternal,	בְּרִיךְ הוּא.

MAY GOD'S NAME BE MADE GREAT AND HOLY   יִתְגַּדַּל וְיִתְקַדַּשׁ שְׁמֵהּ רַבָּא

The word Kaddish (קַדִּישׁ) means "holy" in Aramaic, the language in which the Kaddish is written. The prayer is one of the most important and holiest in our service.

The Kaddish as it is now in our prayerbooks is believed to have been written about twelve hundred years ago, although parts of it are much older than that. The words יְהֵא שְׁמֵהּ רַבָּא מְבָרַךְ לְעָלַם וּלְעָלְמֵי עָלְמַיָּא are based on the Biblical book of Daniel (2:20).

We offer praises although we know that
God is far above mere words of
praise,

  or hymns and blessings

  that we can utter.

  Let us say Amen.

May heaven grant great peace

  and life for us and all Israel.

  Let us say Amen.

May the one who makes peace in the heavens

  make peace

  for us and for all Israel.

And let us say Amen.

לְעֵלָּא מִן כָּל־בִּרְכָתָא וְשִׁירָתָא,

תֻּשְׁבְּחָתָא וְנֶחֱמָתָא,

דַּאֲמִירָן בְּעָלְמָא,

וְאִמְרוּ אָמֵן.

יְהֵא שְׁלָמָא רַבָּא מִן־שְׁמַיָּא,

וְחַיִּים, עָלֵינוּ, וְעַל־כָּל־יִשְׂרָאֵל,

וְאִמְרוּ אָמֵן.

עֹשֶׂה שָׁלוֹם בִּמְרוֹמָיו,

הוּא יַעֲשֶׂה שָׁלוֹם,

עָלֵינוּ, וְעַל־כָּל־יִשְׂרָאֵל.

וְאִמְרוּ אָמֵן.

PRAYER VOCABULARY

Prayer of praise recited in memory of the dead   קַדִּישׁ

May it be made great and holy   יִתְגַּדַּל וְיִתְקַדַּשׁ

And for all Israel   וְעַל־כָּל־יִשְׂרָאֵל

Yigdal is based on Maimonides' Thirteen Principles of Faith. It is a summary of the basic beliefs of Judaism.

Let us tell the greatness of and praise the living God	יִגְדַּל אֱלֹהִים חַי וְיִשְׁתַּבַּח
Who is beyond time and eternal.	נִמְצָא וְאֵין עֵת אֶל מְצִיאוּתוֹ:
God is One and there is no other	אֶחָד וְאֵין יָחִיד כְּיִחוּדוֹ
Who is invisible and measureless.	נֶעְלָם וְגַם אֵין סוֹף לְאַחְדּוּתוֹ:
The Eternal One has no body or form,	אֵין לוֹ דְמוּת הַגּוּף וְאֵינוֹ גוּף
And nothing can be compared to God's holiness.	לֹא נַעֲרוֹךְ אֵלָיו קְדֻשָּׁתוֹ:
The Almighty existed before every thing which was created.	קַדְמוֹן לְכָל־דָּבָר אֲשֶׁר נִבְרָא
As the first to be, but without beginning.	רִאשׁוֹן וְאֵין רֵאשִׁית לְרֵאשִׁיתוֹ:
The Eternal One rules over every creature	הִנּוֹ אֲדוֹן עוֹלָם לְכָל־נוֹצָר
Who reveals God's greatness and majesty.	יוֹרֶה גְדֻלָּתוֹ וּמַלְכוּתוֹ:
The Holy One has given us prophecies	שֶׁפַע נְבוּאָתוֹ נְתָנוֹ
Through those whom God has chosen to be prophets.	אֶל אַנְשֵׁי סְגֻלָּתוֹ וְתִפְאַרְתּוֹ:

THE LAW GOD GAVE WILL NEVER BE CHANGED   לֹא יַחֲלִיף הָאֵל

Some religions believe that the will of God changes. Judaism, however, teaches that the Torah is the Law for all time. It reveals what God expects of us, and it will never be replaced by any other set of laws.

There has never arisen in Israel a prophet like Moses.	לֹא קָם בְּיִשְׂרָאֵל כְּמֹשֶׁה עוֹד
He alone was privileged to see a glimpse of the Almighty.	נָבִיא וּמַבִּיט אֶת־תְּמוּנָתוֹ:
A truthful Torah did the Eternal give to the Jewish people	תּוֹרַת אֱמֶת נָתַן לְעַמּוֹ אֵל
By means of the faithful prophet Moses.	עַל־יַד נְבִיאוֹ נֶאֱמַן בֵּיתוֹ:
The Law God gave will never be changed,	לֹא יַחֲלִיף הָאֵל וְלֹא יָמִיר דָּתוֹ
Nor can it be replaced by any other.	לְעוֹלָמִים לְזוּלָתוֹ:
The Eternal One knows all hidden things	צוֹפֶה וְיוֹדֵעַ סְתָרֵינוּ
And foretells the end of everything even as it begins.	מַבִּיט לְסוֹף דָּבָר בְּקַדְמָתוֹ:
God will reward the person who acts with kindness accordingly	גוֹמֵל לְאִישׁ חֶסֶד כְּמִפְעָלוֹ
And punish the wicked according to his evil behavior.	נוֹתֵן לְרָשָׁע רָע כְּרִשְׁעָתוֹ:
God will send our Messiah at the end of days	יִשְׁלַח לְקֵץ יָמִין מְשִׁיחֵנוּ
To lead all the faithful to salvation.	לִפְדּוֹת מְחַכֵּי קֵץ יְשׁוּעָתוֹ:
The dead will be called to eternal life through God's mercy.	מֵתִים יְחַיֶּה אֵל בְּרֹב חַסְדּוֹ
Blessed be the name of the Eternal forever!	בָּרוּךְ עֲדֵי־עַד שֵׁם תְּהִלָּתוֹ:

PRAYER VOCABULARY	
God is One and there is no other	אֶחָד וְאֵין יָחִיד כְּיִחוּדוֹ
The first to be, but without beginning	רִאשׁוֹן וְאֵין רֵאשִׁית
Like Moses	כְּמֹשֶׁה
Prophet	נָבִיא
God will reward the person who acts with kindness	גוֹמֵל לְאִישׁ חֶסֶד

72

King David was a rich and powerful king. But he was also a good and pious man. In his youth David had been a great and mighty warrior. But in his later years he devoted much of his time to study and prayer.

One day as David was walking in his garden he began to think about his own life and death. "When will I die?" he wondered. "If I knew the time of my death, I would know how to arrange my life to do the most good." David prayed to God. "When will I die?" he asked.

God replied, "No person may know the exact time of his death. I will tell you only that you will die on a Shabbat."

"But I do not want to die on a Shabbat," David said. "Shabbat should be a day of joy. If I die, my friends and family will mourn. Shabbat will be spoiled for them. Please allow me to die on a Friday."

"No," said God. "Your son Solomon is destined to begin his reign on a Sunday. The country cannot be without a king even for one day."

David thought a while and said, "Please allow me to die on a Friday. Then Solomon can become king a day earlier. He will be a good king. He is destined to build the Holy Temple. If he becomes king a day earlier he can begin building your Holy House a day earlier."

God replied, "David, you do not understand. You are a good and pious man. Every Shabbat you spend the day praying to Me and studying Torah. Don't you know that the days you spend praying and studying are worth more than the beautiful sanctuary your son will build?"

—Talmudic Legend

THE SHABBAT MORNING SERVICE
תְּפִלַּת שַׁחֲרִית לְשַׁבָּת

The format and order of the Shabbat morning service
are generally similar to those of the Friday evening
service. It starts with an opening prayer, continues
on to the Shema and its accompanying prayers, then
to the Amidah, and it ends with the concluding prayers.

But there is one important difference in the Shabbat morning service. Between the Amidah and the
concluding prayers, there is the Torah service, in
which the Torah is taken from the Ark and read to the
congregation. In addition, on Shabbat and holidays
there is Musaf, an additional Amidah. So the morning
service for Shabbat has six sections rather than the
four sections of the Friday evening service: the opening prayers, the Shema, the Amidah, the Torah service, the Musaf, and the concluding prayers.

PRAYER VOCABULARY

Morning Service	שַׁחֲרִית
The Opening Prayers (lit. "Morning Blessings")	בִּרְכוֹת הַשַּׁחַר
The Shema and Its Accompanying Blessings	שְׁמַע וּבִרְכוֹתֶיהָ
The Amidah	הַתְּפִלָּה
The Torah Service	קְרִיאַת הַתּוֹרָה
Musaf, additional service	מוּסָף

I. OPENING PRAYERS

מַה־טֹּבוּ אֹהָלֶיךָ

**The service opens with this prayer, which
praises the places where God is worshipped.**

How good are your tents, O Jacob,	מַה־טֹּבוּ אֹהָלֶיךָ יַעֲקֹב,
your places of worship, O Israel.	מִשְׁכְּנֹתֶיךָ יִשְׂרָאֵל.

Blessing before putting on the Tallit

Blessed are You, O Eternal, ruler of the world	בָּרוּךְ אַתָּה יְיָ אֱלֹהֵינוּ מֶלֶךְ הָעוֹלָם
Who has made us holy by Your commandments	אֲשֶׁר קִדְּשָׁנוּ בְּמִצְוֹתָיו
And has commanded us to wrap ourselves in the Tallit.	וְצִוָּנוּ לְהִתְעַטֵּף בַּצִּיצִת.

HOW GOOD ARE YOUR TENTS, O JACOB   מַה־טֹּבוּ אֹהָלֶיךָ יַעֲקֹב

Our ancestors were originally a semi-nomadic people. Their first places of worship were tents. According to tradition, אֹהָלֶיךָ ("your tents") refers to the synagogue, while מִשְׁכְּנֹתֶיךָ ("your places of worship") refers to religious schools where Judaism is taught. Both synagogues and religious schools are necessary to preserve Judaism.

This prayer is a quotation from the Biblical book of Numbers (בַּמִּדְבָּר). We are told that Balak, king of Moab, who hated the Jews, sent a messenger, Balaam, to curse the people of Israel. But Balaam, impressed by the righteousness and piety of the people he had come to curse, blessed them instead with the words of this prayer.

PRAYER VOCABULARY

How good	מַה־טֹּבוּ
Your tents	אֹהָלֶיךָ
Your places of worship	מִשְׁכְּנֹתֶיךָ
To wrap ourselves in the Tallit (lit. "fringes")	לְהִתְעַטֵּף בַּצִּיצִת

In the morning blessings we praise and thank God for having awakened to a new day, refreshed and able to do God's will.

Blessed are You, O Eternal, Ruler of the universe,

בָּרוּךְ אַתָּה יְיָ אֱלֹהֵינוּ מֶלֶךְ הָעוֹלָם

Who has given the mind understanding
to distinguish between day and night.

אֲשֶׁר נָתַן לַשֶּׂכְוִי בִינָה לְהַבְחִין
בֵּין יוֹם וּבֵין לָיְלָה:

Blessed are You, O Eternal, Ruler of the universe,

בָּרוּךְ אַתָּה יְיָ אֱלֹהֵינוּ מֶלֶךְ הָעוֹלָם

Who has made me in Your image.

שֶׁעָשַׂנִי בְּצַלְמוֹ:

Blessed are You, O Eternal, Ruler of the universe,

בָּרוּךְ אַתָּה יְיָ אֱלֹהֵינוּ מֶלֶךְ הָעוֹלָם

Who has made me free.

שֶׁעָשַׂנִי בֶּן חוֹרִין:

Blessed are You, O Eternal, Ruler of the universe,

בָּרוּךְ אַתָּה יְיָ אֱלֹהֵינוּ מֶלֶךְ הָעוֹלָם

Who has made me a Jew.

שֶׁעָשַׂנִי יִשְׂרָאֵל:

TO DISTINGUISH BETWEEN DAY AND NIGHT

The first blessing expresses our thankfulness for the awareness of day and night. The next three praise God for having accorded us the status of free, Jewish people, created in the image of God. Without these blessings from God, we could not stand and praise God and observe the mitzvot.

PRAYER VOCABULARY	
To distinguish	לְהַבְחִין
Between day and night	בֵּין יוֹם וּבֵין לָיְלָה
In the image of God	בְּצַלְמוֹ
Free	בֶּן חוֹרִין

The prayer מַה טֹּבוּ refers to tents and other places where God is worshipped. Jews have worshipped in various kinds of synagogues from the most elaborate and beautiful building to a simple, humble hut; from a tent to a truck outfitted with an Ark and Torah. But all these places of worship have one thing in common: God is worshipped with love and kavanah.

If we were to study synagogues throughout Jewish history, we would see that no particular kind of structure or architecture can be identified as a synagogue building. We can find synagogues that look like forts, like oriental pagodas, like churches, or like cottages. Usually the synagogue was constructed in the architecture of the time and place in which it was built. Often there was nothing on the outside of the building to even indicate that it was a synagogue.

A reconstruction of the famous synagogue at Kfar Nahum.

An open Aron Kodesh.

But although the outside of a synagogue often cannot be distinguished from the outside of any other building, as soon as one steps inside, there is no doubt that one is in a Jewish house of worship. Every synagogue has an Ark (Aron Kodesh) for the Torah and a platform, or bimah, from which the service is conducted. Sometimes the bimah is at the front of the synagogue and sometimes it is in the middle. But it is always raised above the floor.

On the bimah are lecterns or raised desks for the rabbi and cantor, and a table on which the Torah Scroll is placed when it is read.

Many synagogues have beautiful interiors with paintings and stained-glass windows. The decorations often include Menorahs or Ten Commandments. Usually these artistic decorations do not show either animals or people, because many Jews take literally the second commandment, which forbids the making of graven images (idols). However, the ruins of some ancient synagogues show that Jews in earlier times did not interpret this commandment in the same way, since archaeologists have found mosaics in ancient synagogues showing both people and animals.

It is nice to worship in a beautiful synagogue with comfortable seats and beautiful artwork and architecture. But the beauty of the building is not the most important thing. Any place that a minyan (ten or more Jews) gathers to worship God with kavanah is a synagogue. The beauty comes from the sincerity of the worshippers rather than from the physical surroundings.

בָּרְכוּ

The Barchu, or Call to Prayer (p. 37), is the formal opening of the Shabbat morning service as it is of the Friday evening service. The Yotzer Hameorot (Creator of Light) prayer follows the Barchu. Just as in the Friday evening service we thanked God for creating darkness and watching over us at night, we now thank God for creating light and filling the world with so many wonderful things.

יוֹצֵר הַמְאוֹרוֹת

Blessed is the Eternal our God, ruler of the world,	בָּרוּךְ אַתָּה יְיָ, אֱלֹהֵינוּ מֶלֶךְ הָעוֹלָם,
who fashions the light and creates the darkness.	יוֹצֵר אוֹר וּבוֹרֵא חֹשֶׁךְ,
who makes peace and creates everything.	עֹשֶׂה שָׁלוֹם, וּבוֹרֵא אֶת־הַכֹּל.

WHO FASHIONS THE LIGHT AND CREATES THE DARKNESS יוֹצֵר אוֹר וּבוֹרֵא חֹשֶׁךְ

God renews the work of creation every day. Creation is not a finished art, but an ongoing process. According to Jewish tradition, God is always actively concerned with the world. Rather than merely creating the world and then observing it without involvement, God is an active participant, continually guiding the universe.

El Adon is a beautiful hymn which pictures the entire universe singing the praises of God. The poem pictures God enthroned in heaven being exalted not only by the sun, planets, stars, moon, and creatures of the earth, but also by a whole host of heavenly angels singing praises.

The Eternal One is master over all creation.	אֵל אָדוֹן עַל כָּל־הַמַּעֲשִׂים
God is blessed and praised by every living thing.	בָּרוּךְ וּמְבֹרָךְ בְּפִי כָּל־נְשָׁמָה:
God's greatness and goodness fill the universe	גָּדְלוֹ וְטוּבוֹ מָלֵא עוֹלָם
While knowledge and understanding surround God.	דַּעַת וּתְבוּנָה סֹבְבִים אֹתוֹ:
The Exalted One is over all the heavenly angels	הַמִּתְגָּאֶה עַל חַיּוֹת הַקֹּדֶשׁ
Exalted in glory upon the heavenly throne.	וְנֶהְדָּר בְּכָבוֹד עַל־הַמֶּרְכָּבָה:
Purity and justice stand before the throne of the Almighty;	זְכוּת וּמִישׁוֹר לִפְנֵי כִסְאוֹ
Kindness and mercy go before the glory of God.	חֶסֶד וְרַחֲמִים לִפְנֵי כְבוֹדוֹ:
Good are the heavenly lights which God created,	טוֹבִים מְאוֹרוֹת שֶׁבָּרָא אֱלֹהֵינוּ
Formed with wisdom, knowledge, and understanding.	יְצָרָם בְּדַעַת בְּבִינָה וּבְהַשְׂכֵּל:
They are endowed with power and might	כֹּחַ וּגְבוּרָה נָתַן בָּהֶם
To radiate throughout all the world.	לִהְיוֹת מוֹשְׁלִים בְּקֶרֶב תֵּבֵל:

They are filled with splendor and shine brightly.	מְלֵאִים זִיו וּמְפִיקִים נֹגַהּ
Their brilliance is beautiful throughout the universe.	נָאֶה זִיוָם בְּכָל־הָעוֹלָם:
Happy are they in their rising and setting,	שְׂמֵחִים בְּצֵאתָם וְשָׂשִׂים בְּבֹאָם
Obeying the will of their Creator.	עֹשִׂים בְּאֵימָה רְצוֹן קוֹנָם:
Glory and honor they give to God's name.	פְּאֵר וְכָבוֹד נוֹתְנִים לִשְׁמוֹ
In joyous songs of praise they declare God's kingdom.	צָהֳלָה וְרִנָּה לְזֵכֶר מַלְכוּתוֹ:
God called to the sun and it shone forth in light.	קָרָא לַשֶּׁמֶשׁ וַיִּזְרַח אוֹר
God saw it was good and formed the moon.	רָאָה וְהִתְקִין צוּרַת הַלְּבָנָה:

OBEYING THE WILL OF THEIR CREATOR　　עֹשִׂים בְּאֵימָה רְצוֹן קוֹנָם

The composer of this poem looked up to the sky and noticed the brilliance of the stars and planets. He also saw them rise and set regularly, following particular patterns. Here is proof of the wisdom with which God created the entire universe! In El Adon, he pictures the heavenly bodies happily obeying God's will by rising, shining, and setting according to the times established when God set them in place.

PRAYER VOCABULARY

God's greatness and goodness	גָּדְלוֹ וְטוּבוֹ
Fill the universe	מָלֵא עוֹלָם
Kindness	חֶסֶד
Mercy	רַחֲמִים
Heavenly bodies	מְאוֹרוֹת
Sun	שֶׁמֶשׁ
Moon	לְבָנָה

All heavenly bodies give praise to the Almighty.

שֶׁבַח נוֹתְנִים לוֹ כָּל־צְבָא מָרוֹם

All the angels praise God's glory and greatness.

תִּפְאֶרֶת וּגְדֻלָּה שְׂרָפִים וְאוֹפַנִּים וְחַיּוֹת הַקֹּדֶשׁ.

Blessed is the Eternal,

who fashioned the lights.

בָּרוּךְ אַתָּה יְיָ, יוֹצֵר הַמְּאוֹרוֹת.

PRAYER VOCABULARY

Call to prayer	בָּרְכוּ
Who fashions the light	יוֹצֵר אוֹר
And creates the darkness	וּבוֹרֵא חֹשֶׁךְ
Who fashioned the lights	יוֹצֵר הַמְּאוֹרוֹת

אַהֲבָה רַבָּה

The prayer, Ahavah Rabbah, is recited just before the Shema. In it we thank God for so lovingly giving us the precious gift of Torah.

With abundant love You have loved us, O Eternal our God.	אַהֲבָה רַבָּה אֲהַבְתָּנוּ, יְיָ אֱלֹהֵינוּ.
It is more than we deserve. our parent, our ruler	חֶמְלָה גְדוֹלָה וִיתֵרָה חָמַלְתָּ עָלֵינוּ. אָבִינוּ, מַלְכֵּנוּ,
Our ancestors believed in You, and You taught them the laws of life. May You also teach us.	בַּעֲבוּר אֲבוֹתֵינוּ שֶׁבָּטְחוּ בְךָ, וַתְּלַמְּדֵם חֻקֵּי חַיִּים, כֵּן תְּחָנֵּנוּ וּתְלַמְּדֵנוּ.
Let our eyes light up with Your Torah.	וְהָאֵר עֵינֵינוּ בְּתוֹרָתֶךָ,
May our hearts follow Your commandments, and may we love and revere You. We will never be ashamed.	וְדַבֵּק לִבֵּנוּ בְּמִצְוֹתֶיךָ, וְיַחֵד לְבָבֵנוּ, לְאַהֲבָה וּלְיִרְאָה אֶת־שְׁמֶךָ, וְלֹא נֵבוֹשׁ לְעוֹלָם וָעֶד.

WITH ABUNDANT LOVE YOU HAVE LOVED US   אַהֲבָה רַבָּה אֲהַבְתָּנוּ

The theme of this prayer is love, and the prayer begins and ends with the word אַהֲבָה ("love"). God's love for Israel is shown in the teachings of the Torah, and we show our love for God by studying the great teachings of Judaism.

For we, too, trust and love You.

    We are glad when You help us,

Gather us in peace

From the four corners of the earth

And restore us triumphantly to our homeland.

For You are a God of help,

and You have chosen us from all peoples and tongues,

You have brought us close to You

    forever in truth.

    so we can thank You,

    and to lovingly declare Your Unity.

Blessed is the Eternal,

    Who chose the people of Israel with love.

כִּי בְשֵׁם קָדְשְׁךָ הַגָּדוֹל וְהַנּוֹרָא בָּטֶחְנוּ,

נָגִילָה וְנִשְׂמְחָה בִּישׁוּעָתֶךָ.

וַהֲבִיאֵנוּ לְשָׁלוֹם

מֵאַרְבַּע כַּנְפוֹת הָאָרֶץ

וְתוֹלִיכֵנוּ קוֹמְמִיּוּת לְאַרְצֵנוּ

כִּי אֵל פּוֹעֵל יְשׁוּעוֹת אָתָּה,

וּבָנוּ בָחַרְתָּ מִכָּל־עַם וְלָשׁוֹן,

וְקֵרַבְתָּנוּ לְשִׁמְךָ הַגָּדוֹל,

סֶלָה, בֶּאֱמֶת,

לְהוֹדוֹת לְךָ

וּלְיַחֶדְךָ בְּאַהֲבָה.

בָּרוּךְ אַתָּה יְיָ,

הַבּוֹחֵר בְּעַמּוֹ יִשְׂרָאֵל בְּאַהֲבָה.

PRAYER VOCABULARY

With abundant love	אַהֲבָה רַבָּה
Our parent, Our ruler	אָבִינוּ מַלְכֵּנוּ
So we can thank You	לְהוֹדוֹת לְךָ
Who chose the people love of Israel with love	הַבּוֹחֵר בְּעַמּוֹ יִשְׂרָאֵל בְּאַהֲבָה

The Shema for Shabbat morning is the same as for the Friday evening service, but the Mee Chamochah is different.

Who is like You among the mighty, O Eternal?	מִי־כָמְכָה בָּאֵלִים יְיָ?
Who is like You, great in holiness,	מִי כָּמְכָה נֶאְדָּר בַּקֹּדֶשׁ?
awesome in splendor, doing wonders?	נוֹרָא תְהִלֹּת עֹשֵׂה פֶלֶא.
Those who were redeemed sang a new song to You.	שִׁירָה חֲדָשָׁה שִׁבְּחוּ גְאוּלִים לִשְׁמְךָ
On the shore of the sea	עַל־שְׂפַת הַיָּם
they all joined in praising You,	יַחַד כֻּלָּם, הוֹדוּ וְהִמְלִיכוּ
as they said:	וְאָמְרוּ.
"The Eternal will rule forever and ever."	יְיָ יִמְלֹךְ לְעֹלָם וָעֶד.

WHO IS LIKE YOU AMONG THE MIGHTY, O ETERNAL?　　מִי כָמְכָה בָּאֵלִים יְיָ?

These words of praise for God come from the Bible (Exodus 15:11). The first letters of the first four words spell מַכַּבִּי (Maccabee).

PRAYER VOCABULARY

Who is like You	מִי־כָמְכָה
Doing wonders	עֹשֵׂה פֶלֶא
A new song	שִׁירָה חֲדָשָׁה
Those who were redeemed	גְאוּלִים
On the shore of the sea	עַל־שְׂפַת הַיָּם

Throughout the ages God has been called by many names. In this prayer God is referred to as the "Rock of Israel" and the "Holy One of Israel."

Rock of Israel,

    arise and help Israel.

And save Judah and Israel as You

    have promised.

Help us, O Eternal,

    You are the Holy One of Israel.

Blessed is the Eternal

    who redeems Israel.

צוּר יִשְׂרָאֵל,

קוּמָה בְּעֶזְרַת יִשְׂרָאֵל.

וּפְדֵה כִנְאֻמֶךָ

יְהוּדָה וְיִשְׂרָאֵל

גְּאָלֵנוּ יְיָ צְבָאוֹת,

שְׁמוֹ קְדוֹשׁ יִשְׂרָאֵל.

בָּרוּךְ אַתָּה יְיָ,

גָּאַל יִשְׂרָאֵל.

PRAYER VOCABULARY	
Rock of Israel	צוּר יִשְׂרָאֵל
Holy One of Israel	קְדוֹשׁ יִשְׂרָאֵל
Who redeems Israel	גָּאַל יִשְׂרָאֵל

קְדוּשָׁה

Most of the Shabbat morning Tefillah is the same as the Friday evening Tefillah (p. 52). But on Shabbat a special prayer called the Kedushah (Sanctification) is added. It describes the feeling of awe we experience when thinking about God's holiness.

We sanctify Your name throughout the world.	נְקַדֵּשׁ אֶת־שִׁמְךָ בָּעוֹלָם,
As it is sanctified in heaven.	כְּשֵׁם שֶׁמַּקְדִּישִׁים אוֹתוֹ בִּשְׁמֵי מָרוֹם,
As it is written by Your prophet,	כַּכָּתוּב עַל־יַד נְבִיאֶךָ,
They shall call out to each other and say:	וְקָרָא זֶה אֶל־זֶה וְאָמַר:
"Holy, holy, holy is the God of Multitudes.	קָדוֹשׁ קָדוֹשׁ קָדוֹשׁ יְיָ צְבָאוֹת,
All the earth is full of God's glory."	מְלֹא כָל־הָאָרֶץ כְּבוֹדוֹ.

WE SANCTIFY YOUR NAME THROUGHOUT THE WORLD   נְקַדֵּשׁ אֶת־שִׁמְךָ בָּעוֹלָם

This prayer declares the holiness of God. People must also strive for holiness. Jewish philosophers and theologians have taught that Jews have a "mission"—to live lives of such goodness and holiness that they will serve as an example to all mankind.

HOLY, HOLY, HOLY IS THE GOD OF MULTITUDES   קָדוֹשׁ קָדוֹשׁ קָדוֹשׁ יְיָ צְבָאוֹת

The sentence "Holy, holy, holy is the God of Multitudes. The whole earth is full of God's glory" is from the Biblical book of Isaiah (6:3). In it the prophet relates a vision or dream in which God asked him to be a prophet to the Jewish people and bring God's message to them. Isaiah was reluctant at first but then agreed.

Then with loud voices,	אָז בְּקוֹל רַעַשׁ גָּדוֹל
Mighty and strong chorus,	אַדִּיר וְחָזָק מַשְׁמִיעִים קוֹל
The angels say	מִתְנַשְּׂאִים לְעֻמַּת שְׂרָפִים
In resounding praise:	לְעֻמָּתָם בָּרוּךְ יֹאמֵרוּ.
Blessed be the glory of God from heaven.	בָּרוּךְ כְּבוֹד־יְיָ מִמְּקוֹמוֹ:
Reveal Yourself, O Ruler, from Your heavenly place,	מִמְּקוֹמְךָ מַלְכֵּנוּ תוֹפִיעַ
And rule over us, for we wait for You.	וְתִמְלוֹךְ עָלֵינוּ כִּי מְחַכִּים אֲנַחְנוּ לָךְ:
When will You reign in Zion?	מָתַי תִּמְלוֹךְ בְּצִיּוֹן.
Soon, in our days, will You establish Yourself forever.	בְּקָרוֹב בְּיָמֵינוּ לְעוֹלָם וָעֶד תִּשְׁכּוֹן:
May You be exalted and sanctified in Jerusalem, Your city	תִּתְגַּדַּל וְתִתְקַדַּשׁ בְּתוֹךְ יְרוּשָׁלַיִם עִירְךָ
Throughout all generations and for eternity.	לְדוֹר וָדוֹר וּלְנֵצַח נְצָחִים:
And let our eyes see Your kingdom	וְעֵינֵינוּ תִרְאֶינָה מַלְכוּתֶךָ
As was promised in the Psalms	כַּדָּבָר הָאָמוּר בְּשִׁירֵי עֻזֶּךָ
By David, the righteous anointed king:	עַל יְדֵי דָוִד מְשִׁיחַ צִדְקֶךָ
The Eternal shall reign forever.	יִמְלֹךְ יְיָ לְעוֹלָם.
Your God, O Zion, shall rule for all generations. Halleluyah!	אֱלֹהַיִךְ צִיּוֹן לְדֹר וָדֹר. הַלְלוּיָהּ:

From generation to generation,   לְדוֹר וָדוֹר נַגִּיד גָּדְלֶךָ,

    we will proclaim Your holiness   וּלְנֵצַח נְצָחִים קְדֻשָּׁתְךָ נַקְדִּישׁ,

      forever.

    Our praise of You, O God,   וְשִׁבְחֲךָ אֱלֹהֵינוּ

    shall never stop.   מִפִּינוּ לֹא יָמוּשׁ לְעוֹלָם וָעֶד.

For you are a great and holy God and ruler.   כִּי אֵל מֶלֶךְ גָּדוֹל וְקָדוֹשׁ אָתָּה.

Blessed is the Eternal, O holy God.   בָּרוּךְ אַתָּה יְיָ, הָאֵל הַקָּדוֹשׁ.

PRAYER VOCABULARY

Sanctification	קְדוּשָׁה
Holy	קָדוֹשׁ
Zion	צִיּוֹן
From generation to generation	לְדוֹר וָדוֹר

We pray at the conclusion of the Amidah that peace be granted to the people of Israel and to all humanity.

Grant peace, well-being, and blessing in the world	שִׂים שָׁלוֹם טוֹבָה וּבְרָכָה בָּעוֹלָם
with grace, kindness, and mercy,	חֵן וָחֶסֶד וְרַחֲמִים
for us and for all Israel, Your people.	עָלֵינוּ וְעַל כָּל־יִשְׂרָאֵל עַמֶּךָ.
Bless us, O Parent, all of us together	בָּרְכֵנוּ אָבִינוּ כֻּלָּנוּ כְּאֶחָד
with the light of Your presence.	בְּאוֹר פָּנֶיךָ.
For by that light	כִּי בְאוֹר פָּנֶיךָ
You have given us, O Eternal, our God	נָתַתָּ לָּנוּ יְיָ אֱלֹהֵינוּ
a Torah of life, kindness	תּוֹרַת חַיִּים וְאַהֲבַת חֶסֶד
righteousness, blessing, mercy, life, and peace.	וּצְדָקָה וּבְרָכָה וְרַחֲמִים וְחַיִּים וְשָׁלוֹם.
May it be good in Your sight	וְטוֹב בְּעֵינֶיךָ
to bless Your people Israel	לְבָרֵךְ אֶת־עַמְּךָ יִשְׂרָאֵל
at all times with Your peace.	בְּכָל־עֵת וּבְכָל־שָׁעָה בִּשְׁלוֹמֶךָ.
Blessed are You, O Eternal,	בָּרוּךְ אַתָּה יְיָ
Who blesses Your people Israel with peace.	הַמְבָרֵךְ אֶת־עַמּוֹ יִשְׂרָאֵל בַּשָּׁלוֹם:

PRAYER VOCABULARY	
Grant peace	שִׂים שָׁלוֹם
For us and for all Israel	עָלֵינוּ וְעַל כָּל־יִשְׂרָאֵל
Your people	עַמֶּךָ
A Torah of life	תּוֹרַת חַיִּים
At all times	בְּכָל־עֵת וּבְכָל־שָׁעָה
Who blesses	הַמְבָרֵךְ

The synagogue is more than a place of worship. It is also a place of study and learning. Each week a portion of the Torah is read as part of the Shabbat morning service. This helps the worshippers to become familiar with the Torah and understand it.

The custom of reading the Torah publicly began a long time ago in ancient days. Even before there were synagogues, the high priest would read a portion of the Torah to the people in the Bet Hamikdash on Yom Kippur. On some public occasions the Torah was read to the people by the king.

In our own time, there is a reading from the Torah in the synagogue every week. Since the Torah is divided into fifty-four Sidrot, or portions, and one Sidra is read each week (occasionally two Sidrot are read in one week), the congregation reads through the entire Torah in the course of one year. The final portion is read on the holiday of Simchat Torah, but this is not the end of the Torah reading. Just as soon as we finish reading the Torah, we begin it again for the next year. We read the Torah over and over, year after year, because there are always new things to learn, and new things to understand.

PRAYER VOCABULARY	
Synagogue	בֵּית כְּנֶסֶת
Yom Kippur	יוֹם כִּפּוּר
Torah portion	סְדְרָה
The reading of the Torah	קְרִיאַת הַתּוֹרָה

When the Ark was traveling, Moses said,	וַיְהִי בִּנְסֹעַ הָאָרֹן וַיֹּאמֶר מֹשֶׁה
Arise, O Eternal, and disperse Your enemies	קוּמָה יְיָ וְיָפֻצוּ אֹיְבֶיךָ
And cause those who reject You to flee from before You	וְיָנֻסוּ מְשַׂנְאֶיךָ מִפָּנֶיךָ:
For from Zion the Torah will go forth,	כִּי מִצִּיּוֹן תֵּצֵא תוֹרָה
and the word of the Eternal from Jerusalem.	וּדְבַר־יְיָ מִירוּשָׁלָיִם:
Praised be the one who gave the Torah,	בָּרוּךְ שֶׁנָּתַן תּוֹרָה
in holiness to the people of Israel.	לְעַמּוֹ יִשְׂרָאֵל בִּקְדֻשָּׁתוֹ:

PRAISED BE THE ONE WHO GAVE THE TORAH IN HOLINESS TO THE PEOPLE OF ISRAEL

בָּרוּךְ שֶׁנָּתַן תּוֹרָה לְעַמּוֹ יִשְׂרָאֵל בִּקְדֻשָּׁתוֹ

Since the Torah is the central teaching of Judaism, the reading of the Torah is one of the most important parts of the service. It is believed that the practice of reading a portion of the Torah each week was introduced by Ezra the Scribe. Ezra was a Babylonian Jew who returned to Jerusalem when his people were given permission to return to their homeland after the Babylonian Exile. He helped revitalize Judaism and the Jewish community in Jerusalem.

PRAYER VOCABULARY

When the ark was traveling	וַיְהִי בִּנְסֹעַ הָאָרֹן
Arise, O Eternal	קוּמָה יְיָ
And scatter Your enemies	וְיָפֻצוּ אֹיְבֶיךָ
For from Zion the Torah will go forth	כִּי מִצִּיּוֹן תֵּצֵא תוֹרָה
Who gave the Torah	שֶׁנָּתַן תּוֹרָה

שְׁמַע יִשְׂרָאֵל

The Ark (Aron Kodesh) is opened, and as the congregation rises, the Torah is ceremoniously taken out. The reader takes the Torah and recites with the congregation.

Hear, O Israel, שְׁמַע יִשְׂרָאֵל,

the Eternal is our God, יְיָ אֱלֹהֵינוּ

the Eternal is one. יְיָ אֶחָד!

One is our God, אֶחָד אֱלֹהֵינוּ

Great is our Lord, גָּדוֹל אֲדוֹנֵינוּ

Holy is God's name. קָדוֹשׁ שְׁמוֹ:

Tell of God's greatness with me, גַּדְּלוּ לַיְיָ אִתִּי,
and let us praise God's name וּנְרוֹמֲמָה שְׁמוֹ יַחְדָּו.
together.

94

Before each portion of the Sidrah is read, the following blessings are recited. In them we thank God for having given us the Torah. If there is a Bar or Bat Mitzvah, the youngster being honored is called to the Torah and recites the blessings. Often relatives of the Bar or Bat Mitzvah are also given the honor of being called to the Torah to recite the blessings.

Praise the Eternal who is to be praised.	בָּרְכוּ אֶת־יְיָ הַמְבֹרָךְ.
Praised be the Eternal who is to be praised forever and ever.	בָּרוּךְ יְיָ הַמְבֹרָךְ לְעוֹלָם וָעֶד.
Blessed is the Eternal,	בָּרוּךְ אַתָּה יְיָ,
our God, ruler of the world,	אֱלֹהֵינוּ מֶלֶךְ הָעוֹלָם,
who chose us from all other peoples,	אֲשֶׁר בָּחַר בָּנוּ מִכָּל־הָעַמִּים
and gave us the Torah.	וְנָתַן לָנוּ אֶת־תּוֹרָתוֹ.
Blessed is the Eternal, giver of the Torah.	בָּרוּךְ אַתָּה יְיָ, נוֹתֵן הַתּוֹרָה.

BLESSED IS THE ETERNAL, GIVER OF THE TORAH   בָּרוּךְ אַתָּה יְיָ נוֹתֵן הַתּוֹרָה

The blessings that are recited before reading the Torah are very old and go back about 1,000 years. Traditionally, only men were called to the Torah. In many Conservative temples, women are called up as well. The honor of being called to the Torah is called Aliyah.

The Torah scroll is written by hand on parchment with a feather quill. (Those who write Torah scrolls are called scribes.) A great deal of skill and knowledge is required to write a Torah scroll.

PRAYER VOCABULARY

Bar Mitzvah (Son of the commandment)	בַּר מִצְוָה
Bat Mitzvah	בַּת מִצְוָה
The Torah blessings	בִּרְכוֹת הַתּוֹרָה
Who chose us from among all the other peoples	אֲשֶׁר בָּחַר בָּנוּ מִכָּל הָעַמִּים
Giver of the Torah	נוֹתֵן הַתּוֹרָה

After each section of the Torah has been read, the following blessing is recited. It expresses our thankfulness for having the Torah to study, to follow, and to inspire us.

Blessed is the Eternal

    our God, ruler of the world,

    who gave us the Torah of truth,

    and planted eternal life within us.

Blessed is the Eternal,

    giver of the Torah.

בָּרוּךְ אַתָּה יְיָ,

אֱלֹהֵינוּ מֶלֶךְ הָעוֹלָם,

אֲשֶׁר נָתַן־לָנוּ תּוֹרַת אֱמֶת,

וְחַיֵּי עוֹלָם נָטַע בְּתוֹכֵנוּ.

בָּרוּךְ אַתָּה יְיָ,

נוֹתֵן הַתּוֹרָה.

When the Torah reading is finished, the Torah is lifted for all to see and everyone recites:

This is the Torah

Which Moses proclaimed

to the children of Israel

At the command of God through Moses.

וְזֹאת הַתּוֹרָה

אֲשֶׁר־שָׂם מֹשֶׁה

לִפְנֵי בְּנֵי יִשְׂרָאֵל

עַל־פִּי יְיָ בְּיַד־מֹשֶׁה:

PRAYER VOCABULARY	
The Torah of truth	תּוֹרַת אֱמֶת
And planted eternal life	וְחַיֵּי עוֹלָם נָטַע
Giver of the Torah	נוֹתֵן הַתּוֹרָה
This is the Torah	וְזֹאת הַתּוֹרָה
The children of Israel	בְּנֵי יִשְׂרָאֵל

The Haftarah recited after the Torah reading on Shabbat is a portion from one of the books of the prophets. The portion chosen usually expresses or includes an idea or theme related to the content of the Sidra that is read that week.

The exact history of the introduction of a Haftarah portion into the service is not known. However, it is believed that it first became part of the service during the reign of Antiochus, the wicked king of Syria who was the villain of the Chanukah story. As part of his effort to force the Jews to give up their religion and adopt the Greek culture and religion, Antiochus forbade the study and reading of the Torah on pain of death. Although the Jews could no longer read the Torah as part of their service, they continued to read other parts of the Bible that were not forbidden by the decree. After the victory of the Maccabees, they were able to resume the reading of the weekly Torah portion, but they continued the additional readings as well. The additional portions were called Haftarah portions.

In our time the Haftarah is often reserved for the Bar or Bat Mitzvah as part of the celebration, but this was not always so. In some Jewish communities the Haftarah portion was read by a minor (that is, a child under the age of thirteen). In other communities it was chanted as an additional portion by one of those who had been called to the Torah. The custom in Morocco was to call a seven-year-old boy to read the Haftarah. A special ceremony was held in his honor on the Shabbat on which he read the Haftarah for the first time.

PRAYER VOCABULARY	
Portion of the prophets	הַפְטָרָה
Torah portion	סְדְרָה
Torah	תּוֹרָה
Bar Mitzvah	בַּר מִצְוָה
Bat Mitzvah	בַּת מִצְוָה

After the Sidra from the Torah has been read, there is a reading from the prophets called the Haftarah. A special blessing is again recited before the reading. It thanks God for having chosen us to receive the Torah and to be inspired by the truth and righteousness of the prophets.

Blessed is the Eternal

our God, ruler of the world,

who chose good prophets

and has found pleasure in their words

which were spoken in truth.

Blessed is the Eternal,

Who chose the Torah,
Moses the servant of God,

the people of Israel,

and the prophets of truth and righteousness.

בָּרוּךְ אַתָּה יְיָ, אֱלֹהֵינוּ מֶלֶךְ הָעוֹלָם,

אֲשֶׁר בָּחַר בִּנְבִיאִים טוֹבִים,

וְרָצָה בְדִבְרֵיהֶם

הַנֶּאֱמָרִים בֶּאֱמֶת.

בָּרוּךְ אַתָּה יְיָ,

הַבּוֹחֵר בַּתּוֹרָה,

וּבְמֹשֶׁה עַבְדּוֹ,

וּבְיִשְׂרָאֵל עַמּוֹ,

וּבִנְבִיאֵי הָאֱמֶת וָצֶדֶק.

The blessings recited after the reading of the Haftarah express our thanks for the Torah, for the privilege of worshipping God, and for the holiness of Shabbat.

Blessed is the Eternal

    our God, ruler of the world,
    rock of the world,

    righteous one in all generations,

    loyal God,

    who speaks and it is done,

    whose promises are all fulfilled

    in truth and righteousness.

בָּרוּךְ אַתָּה יְיָ, אֱלֹהֵינוּ מֶלֶךְ הָעוֹלָם,

צוּר כָּל־הָעוֹלָמִים,

צַדִּיק בְּכָל־הַדּוֹרוֹת,

הָאֵל הַנֶּאֱמָן,

הָאוֹמֵר וְעוֹשֶׂה,

הַמְדַבֵּר וּמְקַיֵּם,

שֶׁכָּל־דְּבָרָיו אֱמֶת וָצֶדֶק.

For the Torah, for worship, for the prophets,

    and for this Shabbat day

    which You gave us, O Eternal our God,

    for holiness and rest,

    for honor and glory,

    for everything, O Eternal our God,

    we thank You

    and bless You.

עַל־הַתּוֹרָה, וְעַל־הָעֲבוֹדָה, וְעַל־הַנְּבִיאִים,

וְעַל יוֹם הַשַּׁבָּת הַזֶּה

שֶׁנָּתַתָּ לָּנוּ, יְיָ אֱלֹהֵינוּ,

לִקְדֻשָּׁה וְלִמְנוּחָה,

לְכָבוֹד וּלְתִפְאָרֶת,

עַל־הַכֹּל, יְיָ אֱלֹהֵינוּ,

אֲנַחְנוּ מוֹדִים לָךְ

וּמְבָרְכִים אוֹתָךְ.

May Your name be blessed

    in the languages of all people

    forever and ever.

Blessed is the Eternal,

    who makes Shabbat holy.

יִתְבָּרַךְ שִׁמְךָ

בְּפִי כָּל־חַי

תָּמִיד לְעוֹלָם וָעֶד.

בָּרוּךְ אַתָּה יְיָ,

מְקַדֵּשׁ הַשַּׁבָּת.

FOR THE TORAH, FOR WORSHIP, FOR THE PROPHETS

עַל־הַתּוֹרָה וְעַל־הָעֲבוֹדָה וְעַל־הַנְּבִיאִים

The Haftarah reading, which follows the Torah reading, contains a selection from the books of the prophets. Usually the Haftarah reading is related to the Torah reading which it follows. But at certain times of the year the Haftarah reading is appropriate to the season or to a holiday or fast-day of that season. The Haftarah reading is much shorter than the Torah reading, the average length being 21 verses.

The word Haftarah means "dismissal." The portion from the prophets was so called because at one time the service ended, or was "dismissed," after the Haftarah reading.

PRAYER VOCABULARY	
Rock of the world	צוּר כָּל הָעוֹלָמִים
Who speaks and it is done	הָאוֹמֵר וְעוֹשֶׂה
Whose promises are all fulfilled	הַמְדַבֵּר וּמְקַיֵּם
For the Torah	עַל־הַתּוֹרָה
For worship	וְעַל־הָעֲבוֹדָה
For the prophets	וְעַל־הַנְּבִיאִים

As the Torah Scroll is returned to the Aron Kodesh (Ark), we praise God with these verses:

Let them praise the name of the Eternal	יְהַלְלוּ אֶת־שֵׁם יְיָ
for God's name alone is exalted.	כִּי־נִשְׂגָּב שְׁמוֹ לְבַדּוֹ.
God's glory is on earth and in the heavens,	הוֹדוֹ עַל אֶרֶץ וְשָׁמָיִם.
and the rays of glory shine on God's people.	וַיָּרֶם קֶרֶן לְעַמּוֹ,
God's followers,	תְּהִלָּה לְכָל־חֲסִידָיו,
the Children of Israel,	לִבְנֵי יִשְׂרָאֵל
and those near to God,	עַם קְרֹבוֹ,
praise the Almighty. Halleluyah.	הַלְלוּיָהּ.

PRAYER VOCABULARY

Let them praise	יְהַלְלוּ
The Name of the Eternal	אֶת־שֵׁם יְיָ
The Children of Israel	לִבְנֵי יִשְׂרָאֵל

I have given you a good possession. כִּי לֶקַח טוֹב נָתַתִּי לָכֶם,

Do not abandon my Torah. תּוֹרָתִי, אַל־תַּעֲזֹבוּ.

PRAYER VOCABULARY

I have given you a good possession לֶקַח טוֹב נָתַתִּי לָכֶם

Do not abandon my Torah תּוֹרָתִי אַל־תַּעֲזֹבוּ

102

We sing this beautiful prayer as we return the Torah to the Ark.

The Torah is a tree of life	עֵץ חַיִּים הִיא
to those who are firmly devoted to it,	לַמַּחֲזִיקִים בָּהּ
and those who cling to it are happy.	וְתוֹמְכֶיהָ מְאֻשָּׁר.
Its ways are pleasant ways,	דְּרָכֶיהָ דַרְכֵי־נֹעַם,
and all its paths are peace.	וְכָל־נְתִיבוֹתֶיהָ שָׁלוֹם.
Turn us towards You, O Eternal, and we shall return to You.	הֲשִׁיבֵנוּ יְיָ אֵלֶיךָ וְנָשׁוּבָה
Renew our days as of old.	חַדֵּשׁ יָמֵינוּ כְּקֶדֶם:

THE TORAH IS A TREE OF LIFE   עֵץ חַיִּים הִיא

The Torah is referred to as a Tree of Life because it has been an inspiration to Jews through the ages and has given spiritual life to the Jewish people and to Judaism. The prayer is a quotation from Proverbs 3:17, and Lamentations 5:23.

	PRAYER VOCABULARY	
Tree of life		עֵץ חַיִּים
Its ways are pleasant ways		דְּרָכֶיהָ דַרְכֵי נֹעַם
And all its paths are peace		וְכָל נְתִיבוֹתֶיהָ שָׁלוֹם

V. MUSAF AMIDAH

The services which we recite are all reminders of services which were conducted in the Bet Hamikdash. The Musaf is an additional service for Shabbat and holy days. We pray in our Musaf Amidah that God grant us the same spirit of knowledge, reverence for God, and devotion that our ancestors demonstrated when they made their offerings in the Holy Temple. Since we no longer have a Bet Hamikdash, we must be further dedicated to all the mitzvot and especially to rebuilding the Land of Israel.

Musaf begins with the Amidah, the opening paragraphs of which are the same on every occasion: Magen Avraham (p. 52) and Ata Gibor (p. 53).

Kedushah for Musaf describes a vision of God's being praised throughout the universe. The angels in heaven call out to one another: "Holy, holy, holy is the God of Multitudes," and the people on earth recite the Shema twice daily declaring "God is One."

We will worship You and sanctify You	נַעֲרִיצְךָ וְנַקְדִּישְׁךָ
as the holy angels	כְּסוֹד שִׂיחַ שַׂרְפֵי קֹדֶשׁ
who make Your name holy in the sanctuary,	הַמַּקְדִּישִׁים שִׁמְךָ בַּקֹּדֶשׁ.
as described in the prophet's vision:	כַּכָּתוּב עַל־יַד נְבִיאֶךָ.
They called to one another saying:	וְקָרָא זֶה אֶל־זֶה וְאָמַר.
Holy, holy, holy is the God of Multitudes.	קָדוֹשׁ קָדוֹשׁ קָדוֹשׁ יְיָ צְבָאוֹת.
The whole earth is full of God's glory.	מְלֹא כָל־הָאָרֶץ כְּבוֹדוֹ:
All the earth is full of God's glory.	כְּבוֹדוֹ מָלֵא עוֹלָם
God's serving angels ask one another,	מְשָׁרְתָיו שׁוֹאֲלִים זֶה לָזֶה
Where is the place of God's glory?	אַיֵּה מְקוֹם כְּבוֹדוֹ.
In response they give praise:	לְעֻמָּתָם בָּרוּךְ יֹאמֵרוּ.
Praised be the glory of God from heaven.	בָּרוּךְ כְּבוֹד יְיָ מִמְּקוֹמוֹ:
From heaven God will turn in mercy,	מִמְּקוֹמוֹ הוּא יִפֶן בְּרַחֲמִים
and be gracious to the people who proclaim God's unity.	וְיָחוֹן עַם הַמְיַחֲדִים שְׁמוֹ
evening and morning, twice each day,	עֶרֶב וָבֹקֶר בְּכָל־יוֹם תָּמִיד פַּעֲמַיִם
they lovingly recite the Shema:	בְּאַהֲבָה שְׁמַע אוֹמְרִים:

Hear, O Israel, the Eternal is our God, the Eternal is one.

שְׁמַע יִשְׂרָאֵל יְיָ אֱלֹהֵינוּ יְיָ אֶחָד:

The Eternal One is our God, our Parent, our Ruler, our Helper.

הוּא אֱלֹהֵינוּ הוּא אָבִינוּ הוּא מַלְכֵּנוּ הוּא מוֹשִׁיעֵנוּ

In mercy God will announce to us in the presence of all:

וְהוּא יַשְׁמִיעֵנוּ בְּרַחֲמָיו שֵׁנִית לְעֵינֵי כָּל־חָי.

The Almighty will be Your God.

לִהְיוֹת לָכֶם לֵאלֹהִים:

"I am the Almighty, Your God."

אֲנִי יְיָ אֱלֹהֵיכֶם:

As is written in Your holy Bible:

וּבְדִבְרֵי קָדְשְׁךָ כָּתוּב לֵאמֹר.

God will rule forever, Your God, O Zion, for all generations. Praise God.

יִמְלֹךְ יְיָ לְעוֹלָם. אֱלֹהַיִךְ צִיּוֹן לְדֹר וָדֹר. הַלְלוּיָהּ:

Kedushah is followed by Ledor Vador (p. 90)

106

In this paragraph of the Musaf Amidah, we pray that God will restore us to our homeland in Israel.

May it be Your will,	יְהִי רָצוֹן מִלְפָנֶיךָ
Eternal, our God, and God of our ancestors,	יְיָ אֱלֹהֵינוּ וֵאלֹהֵי אֲבוֹתֵינוּ
to lead us joyfully back to our land,	שֶׁתַּעֲלֵנוּ בְשִׂמְחָה לְאַרְצֵנוּ
and establish us within our borders	וְתִטָּעֵנוּ בִּגְבוּלֵנוּ.
where our ancestors brought to You	שֶׁשָּׁם עָשׂוּ אֲבוֹתֵינוּ לְפָנֶיךָ
the necessary sacrifices:	אֶת־קָרְבְּנוֹת חוֹבוֹתֵיהֶם.
The daily sacrifice	תְּמִידִים כְּסִדְרָם
And the additional Musaf offering.	וּמוּסָפִים כְּהִלְכָתָם.

AND ESTABLISH US WITHIN OUR BORDERS וְתִטָּעֵנוּ בִּגְבוּלֵנוּ

The Land of Israel has always held a special place in the hearts of all the Jewish people even when they were exiled from it and could not even visit it. Within its borders stood Jerusalem, the Holy City, and at its center, the Bet Hamikdash, holiest place on earth. Only there were our ancestors able to prepare the daily and Musaf sacrifices that helped bring them to a closer relationship to God.

PRAYER VOCABULARY	
Lead us joyfully back to our land	שֶׁתַּעֲלֵנוּ בְשִׂמְחָה לְאַרְצֵנוּ
Offerings, sacrifices	קָרְבָּנוֹת
Musaf offerings	וּמוּסָפִים כְּהִלְכָתָם

Yismachu (Rejoice) asks God's blessing on all who observe Shabbat and enjoy it.

May those who observe Shabbat rejoice in Your kingdom.	יִשְׂמְחוּ בְמַלְכוּתְךָ שׁמְרֵי שַׁבָּת
May those who delight in the seventh day and make it holy.	וְקוֹרְאֵי עֹנֶג, עַם מְקַדְּשֵׁי שְׁבִיעִי.
May they all know Your goodness.	כֻּלָּם יִשְׂבְּעוּ וְיִתְעַנְּגוּ מִטּוּבֶךָ.
You made the seventh day holy.	וּבַשְּׁבִיעִי רָצִיתָ בּוֹ
It is the most precious day,	וְקִדַּשְׁתּוֹ, חֶמְדַּת יָמִים אֹתוֹ קָרָאתָ,
a reminder of the work of creation.	זֵכֶר לְמַעֲשֵׂה בְרֵאשִׁית.

YOU MADE THE SEVENTH DAY HOLY　　　　　וּבַשְּׁבִיעִי רָצִיתָ בּוֹ וְקִדַּשְׁתּוֹ

Shabbat is a reminder of creation because it celebrates the day of rest after the work of creation was completed (Exodus 20:11). There is a Talmudic legend that when God was in the process of creating the universe, the material world started getting out of control. God called, "Enough! You may go so far and no farther." In the same way, when people find that their small world is getting out of control, they may regain control by means of Shabbat, which is a reminder of God's creation.

PRAYER VOCABULARY	
May they rejoice in it	יִשְׂמְחוּ
The most precious day	חֶמְדַּת יָמִים
A reminder of the work of creation	זֵכֶר לְמַעֲשֵׂה בְרֵאשִׁית

IV. CONCLUDING PRAYERS

The concluding prayers of the Shabbat Musaf Amidah are Retsay (p. 63), Modim (p. 64), and Sim Shalom (p. 91).

The Closing Hymn

One of the following hymns (or another favorite of the congregation) usually concludes the service.

אֵין כֵּאלֹהֵינוּ

This hymn praises God who is unique and supreme.

There is none like our God.	אֵין כֵּאלֹהֵינוּ,
There is none like our holy one.	אֵין כַּאדוֹנֵינוּ,
There is none like our ruler.	אֵין כְּמַלְכֵּנוּ,
There is none like our helper.	אֵין כְּמוֹשִׁיעֵנוּ.
Who is like our God?	מִי כֵאלֹהֵינוּ,
Who is like our holy one.	מִי כַאדוֹנֵינוּ,
Who is like our ruler?	מִי כְמַלְכֵּנוּ,
Who is like our helper?	מִי כְמוֹשִׁיעֵנוּ.
Let us give thanks to our God.	נוֹדֶה לֵאלֹהֵינוּ,
Let us give thanks to our holy one.	נוֹדֶה לַאדוֹנֵינוּ,
Let us give thanks to our ruler.	נוֹדֶה לְמַלְכֵּנוּ,
Let us give thanks to our helper.	נוֹדֶה לְמוֹשִׁיעֵנוּ.

THERE IS NONE LIKE OUR GOD   אֵין כֵּאלֹהֵינוּ

En Kelohenu is a beautiful hymn that is very old. Originally it began with the second verse, "Who is like our God?" This was answered by what is now the first verse, "There is none like our God." In the more recent version found in our Siddur, the first letters of the first three verses spell out אָמֵן (Amen).

The prayer uses four different names for God: אֱלֹהֵינוּ ("our God"), אֲדוֹנֵינוּ ("our holy one," literally, "our Lord"), מַלְכֵּנוּ ("our ruler," literally "our king"), and מוֹשִׁיעֵנוּ ("our helper").

Praised be our God.	בָּרוּךְ אֱלֹהֵינוּ,
Praised be our holy one.	בָּרוּךְ אֲדוֹנֵינוּ,
Praised be our ruler.	בָּרוּךְ מַלְכֵּנוּ,
Praised be our helper.	בָּרוּךְ מוֹשִׁיעֵנוּ.
You are our God.	אַתָּה הוּא אֱלֹהֵינוּ,
You are our holy one.	אַתָּה הוּא אֲדוֹנֵינוּ,
You are our ruler.	אַתָּה הוּא מַלְכֵּנוּ,
You are our helper.	אַתָּה הוּא מוֹשִׁיעֵנוּ.
You are the God to whom our ancestors burnt the fragrant incense (in the Holy Temple).	אַתָּה הוּא שֶׁהִקְטִירוּ אֲבוֹתֵינוּ לְפָנֶיךָ אֶת קְטוֹרֶת הַסַּמִּים.

PRAYER VOCABULARY	
There is no one like our God.	אֵין כֵּאלֹהֵינוּ
There is no one like our holy one.	אֵין כַּאדוֹנֵינוּ
There is no one like our ruler	אֵין כְּמַלְכֵּנוּ
There 's no one like our helper	אֵין כְּמוֹשִׁיעֵנוּ

IV. CONCLUDING PRAYERS עָלֵינוּ לְשַׁבֵּחַ

We bow our heads as we worship and praise God. We pray that one day the entire human race will recognize that there is one God who rules the world.

It is our duty to praise the Master of all
And praise the One

עָלֵינוּ לְשַׁבֵּחַ לַאֲדוֹן הַכֹּל, לָתֵת גְּדֻלָּה

who formed the world in the beginning.

לְיוֹצֵר בְּרֵאשִׁית,

The Eternal has not made us like the nations of other lands.

שֶׁלֹּא עָשָׂנוּ כְּגוֹיֵי הָאֲרָצוֹת,

We are set apart from other families of earth

וְלֹא שָׂמָנוּ כְּמִשְׁפְּחוֹת הָאֲדָמָה,

For our lot is not like theirs, and our destiny is unique.

שֶׁלֹּא שָׂם חֶלְקֵנוּ כָּהֶם וְגוֹרָלֵנוּ כְּכָל הֲמוֹנָם.

So we bow
as we worship and give thanks
to the ruler of rulers,
the Holy One Whom we praise.

וַאֲנַחְנוּ כֹּרְעִים,
וּמִשְׁתַּחֲוִים וּמוֹדִים
לִפְנֵי מֶלֶךְ, מַלְכֵי הַמְּלָכִים,
הַקָּדוֹשׁ בָּרוּךְ הוּא.

As it says in the Torah: God will rule over all the earth.

וְנֶאֱמַר וְהָיָה יְיָ לְמֶלֶךְ עַל־כָּל־הָאָרֶץ

On that day the Eternal will be One

בַּיּוֹם הַהוּא, יִהְיֶה יְיָ אֶחָד,

and God's name will be One.

וּשְׁמוֹ אֶחָד.

WE BOW AS WE WORSHIP   וַאֲנַחְנוּ כֹּרְעִים, וּמִשְׁתַּחֲוִים

In the Alenu it is customary to bow during the recitation of the words וַאֲנַחְנוּ כֹּרְעִים ("We bow").

The Alenu became part of the daily service around the year 1300. It was originally part of the Rosh Hashanah service only. According to some rabbis, it was composed by Joshua when he first entered the Holy Land. Others believe that the author was Rav, a famous rabbi whose opinions are often quoted in the Talmud.

PRAYER VOCABULARY

It is our duty to praise	עָלֵינוּ לְשַׁבֵּחַ
We bow	וַאֲנַחְנוּ כֹּרְעִים
The Holy One Whom we praise	הַקָּדוֹשׁ בָּרוּךְ הוּא
On that day	בַּיּוֹם הַהוּא
The Eternal will be One	יִהְיֶה יְיָ אֶחָד

112

LEARNING MORE ABOUT: A GREAT JEWISH POET

One of the best-known and most popular hymns of the service is Adon Olam (p. 114–115). It is believed that the words to the hymn were written by Solomon Ibn Gabirol, a great Jewish poet who lived in Spain in the eleventh century. Solomon Ibn Gabirol wrote many religious poems in Hebrew that have become part of our service, but Adon Olam is probably the most popular of all.

In addition to his religious poems (called piyutim), Solomon Ibn Gabirol also wrote books on philosophy as well as poems and books on other subjects. One of his most important philosophical books, *Choice of Pearls*, is a collection of wise sayings on various themes. Another book by Ibn Gabirol, *The Fountain of Life*, was translated into Spanish and Latin and became very popular among Christian scholars. Many of them assumed that it

כְּמוֹ הָאֶרְדְמוֹנִי וּמִשְׁלֵי פְלוֹסְפוֹסִים הָרִאשׁוֹנִים וּמוּסָרָם
רִיזָם וְחִידוֹתָם בְּכֹל עִנְיָן שֶׁאָדָם צָרִיךְ אֵלָיו בְּחָכְמַת
סֵר וּבְדֶרֶךְ אֶרֶץ מָסוֹר לִשְׁעָרִים בְּכֹל עִנְיָנִים ..
פֵּירוּשׁ

בְּחַר הַפְנִינִים בַּמְלִיצַת הֵ..חִים הַקַּדְמוֹנִים וְכוֹ פִּי זֶה סֵפֶר
נִקְרָא מִבְחַר הַפְנִינִים לְפִי שֶׁכָּל מִבְחַר הַחָכְמָה שֶׁנִּי יְקָרָה הִיא
לֵית כְּלָוֹם מוּצָא וְנֶחְשָׁב הִיא זֶה הַסֵּפֶר בַּמְלִיצַת חֲכָמִים הֵ
בִּיַּן וְטִירַשׁוֹ דִּבְרֵי מְשָׁלוֹ שֶׁל חָכְמָה שֶׁמָּשָׁלוֹ הַס הַפְלוֹסְפוֹסִי
מָשָׁל הִיא הַדּוּגְמָא וְהַתָּרוֹן הַמָּשָׁל מַשְׁמָעוֹתֵנוּ נִקְרָא מְלִיצָה כ
לְהָכִין מָשָׁל וּמְלִיצָה כוֹ : פְלוֹסְפוֹסִים הַס חַכְמֵי הַיִּשְׁמְעֵאלִי
רִיס לְהָס פְלוֹסוֹפִיס שֶׁמְסַפְרֵי חַכְמֵי הַיִּשְׁמְעֵאלִיס הַכְּתוּבִים
נִתַּק זֶה הַסֵּפֶר וְהֶעֱתַק וְהוּחָלַף לַלָּשׁוֹן הַקֹּדֶשׁ כַּדְּמַיִן לְשׁוֹן ז
נִתְצָא לְשׁוֹנֵנוּ כְּכֹל כְּזֶה הַסֵּפֶר בְּכָמָה מְקוֹמֹת : וּמוּסָרָס וַת
וֹמֵר בְּזֶה הַסֵּפֶר תִּמְצָא מוּסָרָס וּמִדּוֹתָם שֶׁל חַכְמֵי הַקַּדְמוֹנִי

A page from the book "Choice of Pearls," a collection of philosophic writings by Solomon Ibn Gabirol.

had been written by a Christian monk, and before long the author's true identity was forgotten, even among Jews. Hundreds of years afterwards, in the nineteenth century, a scholar discovered that *The Fountain of Life* had been written by Solomon Ibn Gabirol.

Many other writings of Solomon Ibn Gabirol became popular. Some of his piyutim are still part of the service, and other poems and books he wrote are still studied by scholars. But in spite of his great talent, he was very poor. His life was sad and short. He died in 1058 at the young age of thirty-seven.

PRAYER VOCABULARY

Poems	פִּיוּטִים
Solomon Ibn Gabirol	שְׁלֹמֹה אִבֶּן גַּבִּירוֹל

God is ruler of the whole world but watches over each one of us.

The Eternal ruled the world

   before any of the creatures of the earth were created.

אֲדוֹן עוֹלָם אֲשֶׁר מָלַךְ.
בְּטֶרֶם כָּל־יְצִיר נִבְרָא.

When everything was made by God's will,

   God was called the ruler.

לְעֵת נַעֲשָׂה בְחֶפְצוֹ כֹּל,
אֲזַי מֶלֶךְ שְׁמוֹ נִקְרָא,

After everything has come to an end,

   God alone will still rule.

וְאַחֲרֵי כִּכְלוֹת הַכֹּל,
לְבַדּוֹ יִמְלוֹךְ נוֹרָא.

God was, God is, and will remain

   forever glorious.

וְהוּא הָיָה וְהוּא הֹוֶה,
וְהוּא יִהְיֶה בְּתִפְאָרָה.

God is one and there is no other.

   Who can be compared to God?

וְהוּא אֶחָד וְאֵין שֵׁנִי,
לְהַמְשִׁיל לוֹ לְהַחְבִּירָה,

God has no beginning and no end,

   God has strength and power.

בְּלִי רֵאשִׁית בְּלִי תַכְלִית,
וְלוֹ הָעֹז וְהַמִּשְׂרָה.

God is my ruler and my redeemer.

   a rock for my anguish.
   in time of sorrow,

וְהוּא אֵלִי וְחַי גֹּאֲלִי,
וְצוּר חֶבְלִי
בְּעֵת צָרָה.

THE ETERNAL RULED THE WORLD

אֲדוֹן עוֹלָם אֲשֶׁר מָלַךְ.

   God in this hymn is called אֲדוֹן meaning "Ruler" or "Eternal." This name was first given to God by Abraham. The hymn describes God as אֲדוֹן עוֹלָם , the Eternal of the universe who existed before the world began and who will exist forever.

God is my banner and my refuge.

    God helps me when I cry out.

I place my spirit in God's hand

    when I sleep and when I awake.

And with my spirit, my body too.

    The Eternal is with me

    I will not fear.

וְהוּא נִסִּי וּמָנוֹס לִי,

מְנָת כּוֹסִי בְּיוֹם אֶקְרָא.

בְּיָדוֹ אַפְקִיד רוּחִי,

בְּעֵת אִישַׁן וְאָעִירָה,

וְעִם רוּחִי גְּוִיָּתִי;

יְיָ לִי וְלֹא אִירָא.

PRAYER VOCABULARY	
The Eternal of the world	אֲדוֹן עוֹלָם
No beginning	בְּלִי רֵאשִׁית
And no end	בְּלִי תַכְלִית
The Eternal is with me, I will not fear	יְיָ לִי וְלֹא אִירָא

תְּפִלַּת מִנְחָה לְשַׁבָּת

MINCHAH SERVICE FOR SHABBAT

The Minchah service also corresponds to a sacrifice which used to be offered in the Holy Temple. Now it is the last service of Shabbat before darkness begins to fall, signaling the end of the day of rest.

אַשְׁרֵי

Happy are those who dwell in Your temple.	אַשְׁרֵי יוֹשְׁבֵי בֵיתֶךָ
Forever will they praise You.	עוֹד יְהַלְלוּךָ סֶּלָה:
Happy is the people who has this lot.	אַשְׁרֵי הָעָם שֶׁכָּכָה לּוֹ
Happy is the people whose God is the Eternal.	אַשְׁרֵי הָעָם שֶׁיְיָ אֱלֹהָיו.

PRAYER VOCABULARY

Happy	אַשְׁרֵי
Your house	בֵּיתֶךָ
They will praise You	יְהַלְלוּךָ

The Minchah Amidah contains this beautiful middle paragraph which describes the perfect rest we enjoy on Shabbat as a day of delight, peace, tranquility, joy, and renewal.

You are One; Your name is One,	אַתָּה אֶחָד וְשִׁמְךָ אֶחָד.
And who is like Your people Israel	וּמִי כְּעַמְּךָ יִשְׂרָאֵל.
Unique on earth?	גּוֹי אֶחָד בָּאָרֶץ:
A crown of greatness, a crown of salvation,	תִּפְאֶרֶת גְּדֻלָּה. וַעֲטֶרֶת יְשׁוּעָה.
A day of rest and holiness You gave to Your people.	יוֹם מְנוּחָה וּקְדֻשָּׁה לְעַמְּךָ נָתָתָּ:
Abraham was glad;	אַבְרָהָם יָגֵל.
Isaac rejoiced;	יִצְחָק יְרַנֵּן.
Jacob and his sons rested on it.	יַעֲקֹב וּבָנָיו יָנוּחוּ בוֹ:
This day of rest is granted in abundant love.	מְנוּחַת אַהֲבָה וּנְדָבָה.
A rest of true faith,	מְנוּחַת אֱמֶת וֶאֱמוּנָה.
A rest of quiet, peace and tranquility,	מְנוּחַת שָׁלוֹם וְשַׁלְוָה וְהַשְׁקֵט וָבֶטַח.
A perfect rest in which You delight.	מְנוּחָה שְׁלֵמָה שָׁאַתָּה רוֹצֶה בָּהּ.
May Your children know and understand	יַכִּירוּ בָנֶיךָ וְיֵדְעוּ.
That from You comes their rest,	כִּי מֵאִתְּךָ הִיא מְנוּחָתָם.
And by resting they make Your name holy.	וְעַל מְנוּחָתָם יַקְדִּישׁוּ אֶת־שְׁמֶךָ:

PRAYER VOCABULARY

You are One	אַתָּה אֶחָד
And who is like Your people Israel	וּמִי כְּעַמְּךָ יִשְׂרָאֵל
Perfect Rest	מְנוּחַת שָׁלוֹם

HAVDALAH

On Shabbat a wonderful thing happens. A second soul enters the body of every Jew. This is a special spirit that enables each Jew to experience greater joy on Shabbat than can ever be experienced during the ordinary days of the week, when there is work to do and responsibilities to be met. The extra soul inhabits the body throughout the day of Shabbat. It enables the Jew to leave his or her troubles and think of God and the great heritage of Judaism.

But when Shabbat ends, the second Shabbat soul must return to God. It does not want to go. It does not want to leave the wonderful world of Shabbat Shalom (Shabbat peace) and Oneg Shabbat (Shabbat joy). In order to make it easier for the soul to return to heaven, the Jews use sweet-smelling spices in the Havdalah ceremony. The smell of the spices travels up to heaven; the Shabbat soul smells the lovely spices and wants to follow the lovely aroma. So it too goes up to heaven. This makes the trip easier and more pleasant for the reluctant soul.

—Ancient Legend

HAVDALAH

הַבְדָּלָה

At the conclusion of Shabbat, the evening service, Maariv, is said. It includes a paragraph which calls attention to the separation of the Holy Shabbat from the upcoming weekdays. Havdalah then officially declares the end of Shabbat. Havdalah is a very old ceremony. It is believed that it originated over two thousand years ago. At first it was recited in the synagogue. Later, it was introduced as a home observance. Now the Havdalah service is held both in the home and in the synagogue.

There are three important ritual items that are part of the service: a cup of wine, a lighted braided candle, and a spice box filled with sweet-smelling spices. Each has its own special meaning and reason for being part of the ceremony.

In the early days of Jewish history, wine was part of every festive meal. When the ceremony of Havdalah first became popular, it was held at the end of the last Shabbat meal. A cup of wine was customarily drunk at this meal and the blessing was recited. The custom of drinking the wine and reciting the blessing continued even after the Havdalah service was no longer part of the meal.

The spices add a sweet aroma to the ceremony. Long ago it was the custom to purify the air after meals and at other times by tossing a handful of sweet-smelling spices on glowing coals. Of course this could not be done on Shabbat because fire was not allowed. But after the last Shabbat meal was over and Shabbat was concluded, the coals were lit and the spices were thrown on them to purify the air. The sweet and pleasant smell of the spices came to be associated with the conclusion of Shabbat, and a blessing was recited upon smelling the spices. There are also other explanations for the custom of smelling spices at Havdalah, such as the one in the legend at the beginning of this lesson.

The lighted candle represents the first light that is permitted after Shabbat. Since it was forbidden to kindle lights on Shabbat, lighting a fresh light officially marked the end of Shabbat. Jews customarily recite a blessing to indicate their gratitude to the Creator whenever they do something important. The last blessing of the Havdalah ceremony thanks God for creating the light of the fire.

The prophet Elijah has always been a symbol of hope and peace. Just as we welcome the ideals he stands for by opening the door at our Passover Seder and symbolically inviting him in, so do we express our hopes for peace and goodness in the week to come by singing this song about Elijah before the Havdalah service.

The Prophet Elijah, the Tishbee,	אֵלִיָּהוּ הַנָּבִיא, אֵלִיָּהוּ הַתִּשְׁבִּי,
Elijah from Gilead,	אֵלִיָּהוּ הַגִּלְעָדִי.
Speedily in our time	בִּמְהֵרָה בְיָמֵינוּ,
may he come to us	יָבֹא אֵלֵינוּ.
With the Messiah, a descendant of David.	עִם מָשִׁיחַ בֶּן דָּוִד.

PRAYER VOCABULARY

Havdalah	הַבְדָּלָה	The prophet Elijah	אֵלִיָּהוּ הַנָּבִיא
Spices	בְּשָׂמִים	From Gilead	הַגִּלְעָדִי
Havdalah candle	נֵר הַבְדָּלָה	Speedily in our time	בִּמְהֵרָה בְיָמֵינוּ
Wine	יַיִן	May he come to us	יָבֹא אֵלֵינוּ
		The Messiah	מָשִׁיחַ

הַבְדָּלָה

Several ritual objects are an important part of the Havdalah ceremony—a spice box filled with sweet-smelling spices (besamim), a wine cup filled with wine, and a braided candle. The candle is lit and is often given to the youngest person present to hold as the following prayer, expressing our trust in God, is recited.

Behold, God is my deliverer.

הִנֵּה, אֵל יְשׁוּעָתִי,

I trust the Almighty and am not afraid.

אֶבְטַח, וְלֹא אֶפְחָד;

God gives me strength and

כִּי עָזִּי וְזִמְרָת יָהּ, יְיָ,

delivers me.

וַיְהִי לִי לִישׁוּעָה.

In joy we draw water

וּשְׁאַבְתֶּם מַיִם בְּשָׂשׂוֹן,

from the wells of salvation.

מִמַּעַיְנֵי הַיְשׁוּעָה.

God is the deliverer.

לַייָ הַיְשׁוּעָה,

God blesses the people of Israel.

עַל עַמְּךָ בִרְכָתֶךָ, סֶּלָה.

The Eternal, is with us,

יְיָ צְבָאוֹת עִמָּנוּ,

The God of Jacob gives us strength.

מִשְׂגָּב לָנוּ, אֱלֹהֵי יַעֲקֹב, סֶלָה.

The God of all people.

יְיָ צְבָאוֹת,

Happy is the one who trusts the Eternal.

אַשְׁרֵי אָדָם בֹּטֵחַ בָּךְ.

God is our helper.

יְיָ הוֹשִׁיעָה!

God helps us when we call.

הַמֶּלֶךְ יַעֲנֵנוּ בְיוֹם קָרְאֵנוּ.

May we experience light and joy,

לַיְּהוּדִים הָיְתָה אוֹרָה וְשִׂמְחָה,

Happiness and delight.

וְשָׂשׂוֹן, וִיקָר.

So be it with us.

כֵּן תִּהְיֶה לָּנוּ.

We will lift the cup of salvation

כּוֹס יְשׁוּעוֹת אֶשָּׂא,

and call upon Your name.

וּבְשֵׁם יְיָ אֶקְרָא.

The blessings are then recited over the wine, the spices, and the lighted Havdalah candle.

Holding a cup of wine:

Blessed is the Eternal	בָּרוּךְ אַתָּה יְיָ,
our God, ruler of the world,	אֱלֹהֵינוּ מֶלֶךְ הָעוֹלָם,
who creates the fruit of the vine.	בּוֹרֵא פְּרִי הַגָּפֶן.

Over fragrant spices:

Blessed is the Eternal	בָּרוּךְ אַתָּה יְיָ,
our God, ruler of the world,	אֱלֹהֵינוּ מֶלֶךְ הָעוֹלָם,
who creates all kinds of spices.	בּוֹרֵא מִינֵי בְשָׂמִים.

Over a lit Havdalah candle:

Blessed is the Eternal	בָּרוּךְ אַתָּה יְיָ,
our God, ruler of the world,	אֱלֹהֵינוּ מֶלֶךְ הָעוֹלָם,
who creates the light of fire.	בּוֹרֵא מְאוֹרֵי הָאֵשׁ.

WHO CREATES THE LIGHT OF FIRE   בּוֹרֵא מְאוֹרֵי הָאֵשׁ

Havdalah marks the official end of Shabbat. It separates "the holy from the ordinary" and "the light from the darkness." The service contains quotations from the Biblical books of Isaiah, Psalms, and Esther.

PRAYER VOCABULARY	
Havdalah candle	נֵר הַבְדָּלָה
The fruit of the vine	פְּרִי הַגָּפֶן
All kinds of spices	מִינֵי בְשָׂמִים
The light of fire	מְאוֹרֵי הָאֵשׁ

The Havdalah service concludes with a blessing thanking God for separating the holy from the ordinary.

Blessed is the Eternal	בָּרוּךְ אַתָּה יְיָ,
our God, ruler of the world,	אֱלֹהֵינוּ מֶלֶךְ הָעוֹלָם,
who separates the holy from the ordinary,	הַמַּבְדִּיל בֵּין קֹדֶשׁ לְחוֹל,
light from darkness,	בֵּין אוֹר לְחֹשֶׁךְ,
between Israel and other peoples,	בֵּין יִשְׂרָאֵל לָעַמִּים,
the seventh day	בֵּין יוֹם הַשְּׁבִיעִי
and the six days of work.	לְשֵׁשֶׁת יְמֵי הַמַּעֲשֶׂה.
Blessed is the Eternal,	בָּרוּךְ אַתָּה יְיָ,
who separates the holy from the ordinary.	הַמַּבְדִּיל בֵּין קֹדֶשׁ לְחוֹל.

PRAYER VOCABULARY

Who separates	הַמַּבְדִּיל
The holy from the ordinary	בֵּין קֹדֶשׁ לְחוֹל
Light from darkness	בֵּין אוֹר לְחֹשֶׁךְ
Between Israel and other peoples	בֵּין יִשְׂרָאֵל לָעַמִּים
From the six days of work	לְשֵׁשֶׁת יְמֵי הַמַּעֲשֶׂה

תְּפִלּוֹת שׁוֹנוֹת

PRAYERS FOR OTHER OCCASIONS

WEEKDAY PRAYERS

One morning long ago, in a small town in Eastern Europe, two rabbis were having a friendly discussion. Said the first, "Things are not the way they were in my youth. In my day Jews were very religious. They worshipped God with kavanah and love. Now Jews do not care. They pray as an afterthought or not at all. I am very disappointed in my fellow Jews."

"You are wrong," argued the second. "I think the Jews are just as loyal and dedicated as they used to be. They love God in their hearts and never fail to pray."

As the two rabbis walked and argued, they saw a wagon driver repairing a broken wheel on his wagon. As he worked, his lips moved. The rabbis were curious. They approached closer to hear what he was saying and were surprised to discover that he was reciting the morning prayers.

"Aha," said the first rabbi. "You see, I was right. This wagon driver is so concerned with his daily activities that he does not take time out to worship God. So he mumbles his prayers while he is doing his work."

"You are wrong," said the second rabbi. "This wagon driver is so devoted to God that he worships even while doing his daily work."

—Chasidic Story

WEEKDAY PRAYERS תְּפִלּוֹת לְחוֹל

Most Conservative synagogues continue the tradition of holding weekday services. Traditional synagogues still hold services three times a day: in the morning (Shacharit), in the late afternoon (Minchah), and in the evening (Maariv).

The Amidah prayer (often referred to as the Shemoneh Esrey) is an important part of every weekday service. The Amidah recited on weekdays differs from the Shabbat Amidah in that it includes the prayers of petition: prayers in which we ask God for specific things, such as knowledge, understanding, and peace. Some of the prayers of petition are given in this chapter.

PRAYER VOCABULARY	
Morning prayers	שַׁחֲרִית
Afternoon prayers	מִנְחָה
Evening prayers	מַעֲרִיב

The daily weekday morning service (Shacharit) begins with the Mah Tovu, putting on of Tallit and Tefillin (p. 75), continues with the morning blessings (Birchot Hashachar) p. 76, Barchu (p. 37), the blessings (pp. 80, 83–87) of Shema (p. 43–50), and the first two paragraphs of the Amidah (pp. 59–60). Thereafter the following blessings of petition are recited followed by the conclusion of the Amidah (pp.63–4) and Alenu (p. 66). On Monday and Thursday mornings, the Torah is taken out and read (pp. 93, 95–96, 101–3), and Kaddish (pp. 69–70) is recited.

The afternoon (Minchah) service consists of Ashrei (p. 116) and the Amidah for weekdays.

The evening (Maariv) service consists of the Barchu, Shema and its blessings (p. 37–52), the Amidah, and Alenu.

In this prayer we petition for knowledge and understanding:

You give us knowledge
    and teach us understanding.

אַתָּה חוֹנֵן לְאָדָם דַּעַת,
וּמְלַמֵּד לֶאֱנוֹשׁ בִּינָה.

Continue to bless us with knowledge,
    understanding and good sense.

חָנֵּנוּ מֵאִתְּךָ דֵּעָה,
בִּינָה וְהַשְׂכֵּל.

Blessed is the Eternal,
    the gracious giver of knowledge.

בָּרוּךְ אַתָּה יְיָ,
חוֹנֵן הַדָּעַת.

YOU GIVE US KNOWLEDGE   אַתָּה חוֹנֵן לְאָדָם דַּעַת

Knowledge and understanding help us to know what is good and right so that we may fulfill our responsibilities to God and each other and avoid doing wrong.

PRAYER VOCABULARY	
You give us knowledge	אַתָּה חוֹנֵן לְאָדָם דַּעַת
Understanding and good sense	בִּינָה וְהַשְׂכֵּל
The gracious giver of knowledge	חוֹנֵן הַדָּעַת

הָרוֹצֶה בִּתְשׁוּבָה

Here we petition to be allowed to repent:

Our divine parent, return us to Your Torah.

הֲשִׁיבֵנוּ אָבִינוּ לְתוֹרָתֶךָ,

    Our ruler, draw us close to worship You.

וְקָרְבֵנוּ מַלְכֵּנוּ לַעֲבוֹדָתֶךָ.

Bring us back to You in complete repentance.

וְהַחֲזִירֵנוּ בִּתְשׁוּבָה שְׁלֵמָה לְפָנֶיךָ.

Blessed is the Eternal, who accepts repentance.

בָּרוּךְ אַתָּה יְיָ, הָרוֹצֶה בִּתְשׁוּבָה.

BLESSED IS THE ETERNAL, WHO ACCEPTS REPENTANCE

בָּרוּךְ אַתָּה יְיָ, הָרוֹצֶה בִּתְשׁוּבָה

This is a prayer for repentance. When we have strayed from what is right and good, we are sorry, and we pray that we may find our way back to God and a good life.

PRAYER VOCABULARY

Draw us close	קָרְבֵנוּ
In complete repentance	בִּתְשׁוּבָה שְׁלֵמָה
Who accepts repentance	הָרוֹצֶה בִּתְשׁוּבָה.

We petition for forgiveness:

Our divine parent, forgive us, for we have sinned.	סְלַח־לָנוּ אָבִינוּ, כִּי־חָטָאנוּ,
Our ruler, pardon us, for we have done wrong,	מְחַל־לָנוּ מַלְכֵּנוּ, כִּי־פָשָׁעְנוּ.
Because You forgive and pardon.	כִּי־מוֹחֵל וְסוֹלֵחַ אָתָּה.
Blessed is the Eternal, who graciously forgives.	בָּרוּךְ אַתָּה יְיָ, חַנּוּן הַמַּרְבֶּה לִסְלוֹחַ.

OUR DIVINE PARENT, FORGIVE US　　　　　　סְלַח־לָנוּ אָבִינוּ

After repentance comes forgiveness. This prayers asks for forgiveness because we have sinned. The plural *we* emphasizes the sense of community in Judaism. We are each as bad as the worst of us and as good as the best of us.

PRAYER VOCABULARY	
Forgive us	סְלַח לָנוּ
For we have sinned	כִּי חָטָאנוּ
Pardon us	מְחַל־לָנוּ
Who graciously forgives	חַנּוּן הַמַּרְבֶּה לִסְלוֹחַ

We pray for health:

O Eternal, heal us and we shall be healed.

רְפָאֵנוּ יְיָ וְנֵרָפֵא.

Save us and we shall be saved

הוֹשִׁיעֵנוּ וְנִוָּשֵׁעָה.

For to You we offer praise.

כִּי תְהִלָּתֵנוּ אָתָּה.

Grant us a complete cure for all our ailments.

וְהַעֲלֵה רְפוּאָה שְׁלֵמָה לְכָל־מַכּוֹתֵינוּ.

For You, O God, are our Ruler a faithful and merciful healer,

כִּי אֵל מֶלֶךְ רוֹפֵא נֶאֱמָן וְרַחֲמָן אָתָּה.

Blessed is the Eternal.

בָּרוּךְ אַתָּה יְיָ.

Who cures the sick among the people of Israel.

רוֹפֵא חוֹלֵי עַמּוֹ יִשְׂרָאֵל.

O ETERNAL, HEAL US AND WE SHALL BE HEALED   רְפָאֵנוּ יְיָ וְנֵרָפֵא

We all fear illness and pain. We pray for good health and a cure for all our ills.

PRAYER VOCABULARY

O Eternal, heal us	רְפָאֵנוּ יְיָ
A complete cure	רְפוּאָה שְׁלֵמָה
Who cures the sick	רוֹפֵה חוֹלֵי
among the people of Israel.	עַמּוֹ יִשְׂרָאֵל

We pray for freedom:

Sound the great Shofar to proclaim freedom.	תְּקַע בְּשׁוֹפָר גָּדוֹל לְחֵרוּתֵנוּ,
Raise the banner to assemble our exiles,	וְשָׂא נֵס לְקַבֵּץ גָּלֻיּוֹתֵנוּ.
and gather us together from the four corners of the earth.	וְקַבְּצֵנוּ יַחַד מֵאַרְבַּע כַּנְפוֹת הָאָרֶץ.
Blessed are You, O Eternal, Who will gather the dispersed of Your people Israel.	בָּרוּךְ אַתָּה יְיָ מְקַבֵּץ נִדְחֵי עַמּוֹ יִשְׂרָאֵל:

SOUND THE GREAT SHOFAR TO PROCLAIM FREEDOM   תְּקַע בְּשׁוֹפָר גָּדוֹל לְחֵרוּתֵנוּ

In many periods of history Jews were not free. But they always longed for freedom. Today, in our country, Jews enjoy greater freedom than in any other period of history. Many Jews dedicate themselves to work for freedom for those who are not as fortunate.

PRAYER VOCABULARY	
Sound the Shofar	תְּקַע בְּשׁוֹפָר
From the four corners of the world	מֵאַרְבַּע כַּנְפוֹת הָאָרֶץ

We petition that our prayers be accepted:

Hear our voice, O Eternal our God,

שְׁמַע קוֹלֵנוּ, יְיָ אֱלֹהֵינוּ.

Have mercy on us and favor us.

חוּס וְרַחֵם עָלֵינוּ.

Accept our prayers with mercy.

וְקַבֵּל בְּרַחֲמִים וּבְרָצוֹן אֶת־תְּפִלָּתֵנוּ.

Because You are a God

כִּי־אֵל שׁוֹמֵעַ תְּפִלּוֹת וְתַחֲנוּנִים אָתָּה,

    who hears pleas and prayers.

    Please do not turn away from us.

וּמִלְּפָנֶיךָ מַלְכֵּנוּ רֵיקָם אַל־תְּשִׁיבֵנוּ,

    Listen to the prayers of Your people

כִּי אַתָּה שׁוֹמֵעַ תְּפִלַּת

    Israel with great mercy.

עַמְּךָ יִשְׂרָאֵל בְּרַחֲמִים.

Blessed is the Eternal, who hears prayers.

בָּרוּךְ אַתָּה יְיָ, שׁוֹמֵעַ תְּפִלָּה.

PRAYER VOCABULARY	
Hear our voice	שְׁמַע קוֹלֵנוּ
Have mercy on us	רַחֵם עָלֵינוּ.
Who hears prayers	שׁוֹמֵעַ תְּפִלָּה

FOCUS ON:
THE IDEALS OF THE JEWISH PEOPLE

In addition to containing the order and procedure for worshipping God, the prayerbook teaches us many lessons about Judaism and the Jewish people. For example, by reading the paragraphs of the Amidah, we can learn about some of the things that were important to our ancestors. Many of the prayers were not for tangible things, such as health and prosperity, but express, instead, lofty ideals and hopes to benefit all mankind.

There are prayers for justice. In many periods of Jewish history, governments were corrupt and laws were unfair. The Jews longed for justice for themselves and for all people, and they prayed for it in their prayers.

There are prayers for freedom. Freedom has always been an ideal in Judaism. It goes back to the days of slavery in Egypt and the liberation of the Jews from bondage. Whenever the Jews were not free they prayed for freedom for themselves and all people. Even in good times of freedom, the Jews did not forget that others in the world were enslaved.

The last blessing in the Amidah is a blessing for peace. This has always been one of the greatest goals of the Jewish people. Many prayers throughout the service express the great yearning of the Jews for a world of peace and blessing for all people.

The Liberty Bell in Philadelphia. The inscription on the bell is from the third book of the Bible, Leviticus XXV:10, reading "Proclaim liberty throughout the land, unto all the inhabitants thereof."

PRAYER VOCABULARY	
Ancestors	אָבוֹת
Justice	צְדָקָה
Freedom	חֵרוּת
Peace	שָׁלוֹם

136

HIGH HOLY DAY PRAYERS

On Rosh Hashanah God judges all the people in the world. After evaluating each person's record, God writes the verdict in one of three books arranged on a table before the heavenly throne. The first book is for the names of those who are completely wicked. They will be punished in the year to come. The second book is for the names of those who are completely good and righteous. They will be rewarded in the year to come. The third and largest book is for the names of all other people—those who are not completely good or completely evil. God does not decide about these people until Yom Kippur, when the final verdict is sealed. During the Ten Days of Penitence they have a chance to repent for all their sins and to show God that they are worthy of a good year.

—Talmudic Legend

Rosh Hashanah is the New Year, a solemn time of prayer for Jews. It is a time of self-evaluation and repentance. Although most Jews no longer believe that God literally writes our individual destinies in a Book of Life or a Book of Death, this idea forms the basis for many of the prayers of this season.

And we greet our fellow-Jews with a special greeting that has the theme of Rosh Hashanah in it.

May you be inscribed for a Happy Year.   לְשָׁנָה טוֹבָה תִּכָּתֵבוּ.

PRAYER VOCABULARY	
New Year	רֹאשׁ הַשָּׁנָה
Book of Life	סֵפֶר חַיִּים
Prayers	תְּפִלוֹת

In this prayer we ask God to inscribe us in the Book of Life.

Remember us for life,	זָכְרֵנוּ לְחַיִּים,
O ruler who wants to give life,	מֶלֶךְ חָפֵץ בַּחַיִּים,
and write us in the Book of Life,	וְכָתְבֵנוּ בְּסֵפֶר הַחַיִּים,
for Your sake, God of life.	לְמַעַנְךָ אֱלֹהִים חַיִּים.

Who can be compared to You, Merciful One?	מִי כָמוֹךָ אַב הָרַחֲמִים
In mercy You remember Your creatures with life.	זוֹכֵר יְצוּרָיו לְחַיִּים בְּרַחֲמִים:

O RULER WHO WANTS TO GIVE LIFE מֶלֶךְ חָפֵץ בַּחַיִּים

God is characterized as a ruler (literally as a king) who wants to give life (חָפֵץ בַּחַיִּים). Jews believe that God is generous and kind and loves humankind.

PRAYER VOCABULARY

Remember us to life	זָכְרֵנוּ לְחַיִּים
In the Book of Life	בְּסֵפֶר הַחַיִּים
For Your sake	לְמַעַנְךָ

We also ask for peace and prosperity.

May we be remembered in the Book of Life, Blessing, Peace and Prosperity,	בְּסֵפֶר חַיִּים, בְּרָכָה וְשָׁלוֹם וּפַרְנָסָה טוֹבָה, נִזָּכֵר
and may we and all Israel be inscribed	וְנִכָּתֵב לְפָנֶיךָ, אֲנַחְנוּ וְכָל־עַמְּךָ בֵּית יִשְׂרָאֵל,
for a good life and for peace.	לְחַיִּים טוֹבִים וּלְשָׁלוֹם.
Blessed is the Eternal,	בָּרוּךְ אַתָּה יְיָ,
who makes peace.	עוֹשֶׂה הַשָּׁלוֹם.

בְּסֵפֶר חַיִּים בְּרָכָה וְשָׁלוֹם וּפַרְנָסָה טוֹבָה

IN THE BOOK OF LIFE, BLESSING, PEACE, AND PROSPERITY

Second only to our desire for life is our desire for peace (שָׁלוֹם). God is a God of peace. Peace refers not only to peace between nations, but also to peace and goodwill between persons.

PRAYER VOCABULARY

Book of Lite	סֵפֶר חַיִּים
Who makes peace	עוֹשֶׂה הַשָּׁלוֹם
Prosperity	וּפַרְנָסָה טוֹבָה
For a good life	לְחַיִּים טוֹבִים

אָבִינוּ מַלְכֵּינוּ

**We imagine God as a loving parent and kind ruler as
we plead for mercy and a good year.**

Our divine Parent, our Ruler, we have
no Ruler other than You.

אָבִינוּ מַלְכֵּינוּ, אֵין לָנוּ מֶלֶךְ אֶלָּא
אָתָּה.

Our divine Parent, our Ruler, help us
for Your own sake.

אָבִינוּ מַלְכֵּינוּ, עֲשֵׂה עִמָּנוּ לְמַעַן
שְׁמֶךָ.

Our divine Parent, our Ruler, grant us
a good new year.

אָבִינוּ מַלְכֵּנוּ חַדֵּשׁ עָלֵינוּ שָׁנָה
טוֹבָה.

Our divine Parent, our Ruler, forgive
and pardon all our sins.

אָבִינוּ מַלְכֵּינוּ, סְלַח וּמְחַל
לְכָל־עֲווֹנוֹתֵינוּ.

Our divine Parent, our Ruler, help us
return with complete repentance to
You.

אָבִינוּ מַלְכֵּינוּ, הַחֲזִירֵנוּ בִּתְשׁוּבָה
שְׁלֵמָה לְפָנֶיךָ.

Our divine Parent, our Ruler, inscribe
us in the book of good life.

אָבִינוּ מַלְכֵּינוּ, כָּתְבֵנוּ בְּסֵפֶר חַיִּים
טוֹבִים:

Our divine Parent, our Ruler, answer
us though we have no deeds to plead
our cause, treat us with mercy and
kindness and save us.

אָבִינוּ מַלְכֵּינוּ, חָנֵּנוּ וַעֲנֵנוּ, כִּי
אֵין בָּנוּ מַעֲשִׂים, עֲשֵׂה עִמָּנוּ צְדָקָה
וָחֶסֶד וְהוֹשִׁיעֵנוּ.

OUR DIVINE PARENT　　　　　　　　　　　אָבִינוּ מַלְכֵּנוּ

God is not only our ruler (מַלְכֵּנוּ) but also our parent (אָבִינוּ). As we think about our
life in the year that just passed, and think ahead to our life in the year to come, we long for
a God who is loving and forgiving as a parent—a God with whom we have a warm, close
personal relationship.

PRAYER VOCABULARY	
Our divine Parent, our Ruler	אָבִינוּ מַלְכֵּנוּ
A good new year	שָׁנָה טוֹבָה
Forgive	סְלַח
Repentance	תְשׁוּבָה
Inscribe us	כָּתְבֵנוּ
Treat us with mercy and kindness	עֲשֵׂה עִמָּנוּ צְדָקָה וָחֶסֶד
And save us	וְהוֹשִׁיעֵנוּ
Who kept us alive	שֶׁהֶחֱיָנוּ

An important part of the Rosh Hashanah service is the blowing of the shofar, the ram's horn. Before the shofar is blown a special blessing is recited.

Blessed is the Eternal

    our God, ruler of the world,

    who made us holy by the mitzvot

    and commanded us to listen to the sound of the shofar.

בָּרוּךְ אַתָּה יְיָ,

אֱלֹהֵינוּ מֶלֶךְ הָעוֹלָם,

אֲשֶׁר קִדְּשָׁנוּ בְּמִצְוֹתָיו,

וְצִוָּנוּ לִשְׁמֹעַ קוֹל שׁוֹפָר.

Blessed is the Eternal

    our God, ruler of the world,

    who kept us alive and well,

    and gave us the opportunity, to celebrate this occasion.

בָּרוּךְ אַתָּה יְיָ,

אֱלֹהֵינוּ מֶלֶךְ הָעוֹלָם,

שֶׁהֶחֱיָנוּ וְקִיְּמָנוּ

וְהִגִּיעָנוּ לַזְּמַן הַזֶּה.

AND COMMANDED US TO LISTEN TO THE SOUND OF THE SHOFAR וְצִוָּנוּ לִשְׁמֹעַ קוֹל שׁוֹפָר

One of the names for Rosh Hashanah is Yom Teruah (יוֹם תְּרוּעָה), the Day of Blowing the Shofar. This is the Biblical name of the holiday. According to our tradition, the Shofar was blown at Mount Sinai to announce the giving of the Torah. It is blown on Rosh Hashanah to announce the New Year and remind us of our great heritage.

PRAYER VOCABULARY	
Ram's horn	שׁוֹפָר
To listen to	לִשְׁמֹעַ
The sound of the shofar	קוֹל שׁוֹפָר

Yom Kippur is the most sacred day of the Jewish year. It is called the Sabbath of Sabbaths because it is more holy even than Shabbat, which is considered the second-most-important day of the Jewish year. According to tradition, Yom Kippur is the day of final judgement, the day on which God seals the fate of each Jew for the coming year.

Yom Kippur is devoted to prayer and to fasting. We do not fast in order to punish ourselves, but to enable us to concentrate on the meaning of Yom Kippur. By abstaining from food, we concentrate only on the loftiness of this day—the holiest in the Jewish calendar.

PRAYER VOCABULARY

Day of Atonement	יוֹם כִּפּוּר
Sabbath of Sabbaths	שַׁבַּת שַׁבָּתוֹן
Fast	צוֹם

The service on the evening of Yom Kippur is often called the Kol Nidre service, or just Kol Nidre. It takes its name from the Kol Nidre prayer, sung by the cantor to a hauntingly beautiful melody as the service opens. This prayer is so important that it has given its name to the entire service in which it occurs. This is the only night of the year on which the Tallit is worn. The Kol Nidre prayer is largely in Aramaic, the same language in which the Kaddish is written.

All the promises,   כָּל נִדְרֵי,

    pledges, and oaths   וֶאֱסָרֵי, וַחֲרָמֵי, וְקוֹנָמֵי,

                    וְכִנּוּיֵי, וְקִנּוּסֵי, וּשְׁבוּעוֹת,

which we promise without   דְּנָדַרְנָא, וּדְאִשְׁתְּבַּעְנָא, וּדְאַחֲרִימְנָא,
thinking or meaning to,

may we be forgiven for them,   וּדְאָסַרְנָא עַל נַפְשָׁתָנָא.
and good come to us .

From this Yom Kippur   מִיוֹם כִּפֻּרִים זֶה,

    until next Yom Kippur.   עַד יוֹם כִּפֻּרִים הַבָּא עָלֵינוּ לְטוֹבָה.

ALL THE PROMISES, PLEDGES, AND OATHS   כָּל נִדְרֵי, וֶאֱסָרֵי, וַחֲרָמֵי

    In the fifteenth century in Spain, Jews were persecuted by the Christian Church. Many were forced to convert to Christianity. If they refused, they were killed or exiled. Many Jews pretended to renounce their religion and took oaths of loyalty to Christianity. But they remained Jews in secret. On Yom Kippur they nullified their oaths of loyalty and prayed to be forgiven.

PRAYER VOCABULARY

Day of Atonement	יוֹם כִּפּוּר
All the promises	כָּל נִדְרֵי

If we truly atone—if we are truly sorry for the wrongs we have done—God will accept our prayers. This statement comes from the Torah (Leviticus 16:30) and describes the atonement service in the Holy Temple.

On this day, your atonement	כִּי בַיּוֹם הַזֶּה יְכַפֵּר עֲלֵיכֶם,
will purify you from your sins.	לְטַהֵר אֶתְכֶם מִכֹּל חַטֹּאתֵיכֶם,
You will be pure before God.	לִפְנֵי יְיָ תִּטְהָרוּ.

כִּי בַיּוֹם הַזֶּה יְכַפֵּר עֲלֵיכֶם לְטַהֵר אֶתְכֶם מִכֹּל חַטֹּאתֵיכֶם

ON THIS DAY, YOUR ATONEMENT WILL PURIFY YOU FROM YOUR SINS

Jews believe that only sins against God can be forgiven by God and that it is for those sins that we atone in prayer. But sins against our fellow human beings can be forgiven by God only after we have asked forgiveness from those against whom we sinned.

PRAYER VOCABULARY

On this day	כִּי בַיּוֹם הַזֶּה
Will purify you	לְטַהֵר אֶתְכֶם
From all your sins	מִכָּל חַטֹּאתֵיכֶם

עַל חֵטְא

Jews pray as a community. They pray not only for themselves, but for the entire Jewish people. The Al Chet prayer is a confession of sins, not only sins committed personally by those who are saying the prayer, but also sins that may have been committed by other members of the Jewish community. As you read this prayer you will realize that you are asking forgiveness for many sins which you yourself have never committed. But remember that you are asking for forgiveness not only for yourself, but for all your fellow Jews.

For the sins we committed
    that we did not mean, and for
       those we committed voluntarily.

עַל חֵטְא שֶׁחָטָאנוּ לְפָנֶיךָ,

בְּאֹנֶס וּבְרָצוֹן.

For the sins we committed without knowing.

עַל חֵטְא שֶׁחָטָאנוּ לְפָנֶיךָ בִּבְלִי דָעַת.

For the sins we committed knowingly and dishonestly.

עַל חֵטְא שֶׁחָטָאנוּ לְפָנֶיךָ בְּדַעַת וּבְמִרְמָה.

For the sins we committed by cheating others.

עַל חֵטְא שֶׁחָטָאנוּ לְפָנֶיךָ בְּהוֹנָאַת רֵעַ,

For the sins we committed by being disrespectful to parents and teachers.

עַל חֵטְא שֶׁחָטָאנוּ לְפָנֶיךָ בְּזִלְזוּל הוֹרִים וּמוֹרִים,

For the sins we committed by using violence.

עַל חֵטְא שֶׁחָטָאנוּ לְפָנֶיךָ בְּחֹזֶק יָד.

For the sins we committed by using bad language.

עַל חֵטְא שֶׁחָטָאנוּ לְפָנֶיךָ בְּטֻמְאַת שְׂפָתָיִם,

For the sins we committed by not resisting temptation.

עַל חֵטְא שֶׁחָטָאנוּ לְפָנֶיךָ בְּיֵצֶר הָרָע.

FOR THE SINS WE COMMITTED   עַל חֵטְא שֶׁחָטָאנוּ לְפָנֶיךָ

    In some religions confession takes place in secret, but not in Judaism. In this prayer we confess our sins openly and ask that they be forgiven. However, we cannot confess, beg forgiveness, and then continue to commit the same wrongs. Confession must be accompanied by a sincere desire to change our wrongful behavior.

For all of these, God of forgiveness,

forgive us, pardon us,

and let us atone.

וְעַל כֻּלָּם, אֱלֽוֹהַּ סְלִיחוֹת,
סְלַח לָֽנוּ, מְחַל לָֽנוּ,
כַּפֶּר־לָֽנוּ.

PRAYER VOCABULARY

For the sins	עַל חֵטְא
We committed	שֶׁחָטָֽאנוּ
By acting violently	בְּחֹֽזֶק יָד
Parents	הוֹרִים
And teachers	וּמוֹרִים
Forgive us	סְלַח לָֽנוּ

Jews believe that God will only forgive those sins that a person commits against God. Sins committed by one person against another must first be forgiven by the person who was wronged. Only then will God grant forgiveness.

In the Middle Ages it was the custom for each family to bring a lighted candle to the synagogue on Yom Kippur eve.

The candles provided light for those congregants who wished to remain in the synagogue all night to study or pray.

Some Jews observe the custom of beginning to build a sukkah for Sukkot as soon as the Yom Kippur service is over. In that way they do not waste any time after one mitzvah is completed before beginning the next one.

SOMETHING TO THINK ABOUT

In order to emphasize that every action of every human being has moral significance, the rabbis of the Talmud taught that we should always behave as if we thought that our good deeds and our bad deeds were equally balanced. Thus, if we commit a good deed, we are swinging the scale of judgment toward the side of good, and if we commit a bad deed, we are tilting it toward the side of evil. The world too, they said, should be seen as evenly balanced between good and evil. From this perspective, our actions as individuals determine not only whether our own life stands on the side of good or evil, but whether the entire world is good or evil.

Yizkor is a special prayer recited on Yom Kippur. The name of this prayer means "memorial," and it is said by everyone who has ever lost a loved one, such as a parent, child, husband, wife, brother, or sister, not just during the preceding year, as for Kaddish, but at any time. The loved one's name and relationship to the mourner are mentioned as part of the prayer.

Saying Yizkor helps us to remember the special feelings we had for loved ones who no longer share our lives. Although the prayer makes us sad, remembering the good times we shared with those who are now dead, it helps to relieve some of the sadness and makes us grateful that we had the opportunity to know and love them.

Another way of remembering close relatives who have died is by lighting a memorial candle on the evening of Yom Kippur. This is the same type of candle that is lit on the anniversary, or Yahrzeit, of the death of a loved one.

By reciting the Yizkor prayer and lighting the memorial candle, we are saying that even though death is sad, and we will always miss our loved ones who die, we are glad to be alive and are grateful for God's goodness to us.

PRAYER VOCABULARY

Memorial prayer	יִזְכּוֹר
Kaddish	קַדִּישׁ
Yahrzeit (lit. "Anniversary" in Yiddish)	יָאהרְצַייט

THE THREE PILGRIMAGE FESTIVALS

Rabbi Yochanan, an aged and famous rabbi of ancient times, was taking a walk with his young friend, Rabbi Hiyya. Rabbi Hiyya walked tall and straight, while Rabbi Yochanan, who was stooped and bent with age, leaned on his arm. Soon they came to a farm. Rabbi Yochanan said to his friend, "I used to own this farm, but I sold it. I did not want to spend the time it took to take care of it. I wanted to have the extra time to devote to studying Torah." As they walked farther, they came to a vineyard. Again Rabbi Yochanan said to his friend, "This vineyard used to be mine, but I sold it so that I would have more time to devote to studying Torah." The two continued walking until they came to an olive orchard. Again Rabbi Yochanan said, "This orchard belonged to me, but I sold it so that I would have more time to study Torah."

As young Rabbi Hiyya listened to his aged friend, he began to cry. "Why are you crying?" asked Rabbi Yochanan. "I am crying because you gave up all your material possessions and you will have nothing left for your old age."

"Foolish young man," said Rabbi Yochanan. "Do not cry. I gave up my material possessions it is true. But I kept a more precious possession, my spiritual heritage. The study of Torah is more important to God than the entire world. It took the Almighty only six days to create the world, but it took forty days and nights to pass the Torah down to Moses so that he could teach it to the Jewish people. That is why the study of Torah is more important than all the worldly possessions."

Other than Rosh Hashanah and Yom Kippur, the only holidays that Jews are commanded to observe in the Torah are Passover, Sukkot, and Shavuot. These are called the three pilgrimage holidays, because in ancient times they were the occasions when Jews journeyed from the far corners of their country to the Temple (Bet Hamikdash) to sacrifice to God.

Each of the pilgrimage holidays has two meanings. They are important, first of all, as harvest festivals. In ancient times the Jews of Eretz Yisrael thanked God for an abundant harvest by bringing the first of their crops to the Bet Hamikdash at each pilgrimage festival. Today in modern Israel many Jews are farming the land once again. During the changing agricultural seasons we pray for rain and sunshine at the appropriate times for Israel to insure a good crop.

The three holidays also commemorate major events in the history and religious life of the Jews. The holiday of Passover commemorates the exodus from slavery in Egypt. The holiday of Sukkot reminds us of the temporary shelters the Jews built as they wandered through the desert, and the holiday of Shavuot memorializes the greatest religious experience in Jewish history—the giving of the Torah on Mount Sinai.

PRAYER VOCABULARY

Three Pilgrimage Festivals	שָׁלֹשׁ רְגָלִים
Holiday of Passover	פֶּסַח
Holiday of Sukkot	סֻכּוֹת
Holiday of Shavuot	שָׁבוּעוֹת
Holy Temple	בֵּית הַמִקְדָּשׁ
Rain	גֶשֶׁם
Booth	סֻכָּה
Mount Sinai	הַר סִינַי

הַדְלָקַת הַנֵּרוֹת לְשָׁלֹשׁ רְגָלִים

The festivals begin, as does Shabbat, with the lighting of candles and the reciting of the blessing. The festival blessing is very similar to the Shabbat candle blessing, but instead of thanking God for commanding us to light candles for Shabbat, we thank God for commanding us to light candles on the festival.

The candle blessing is followed by the Shehecheyanu, in which we thank God for enabling us to be alive and well and to have the opportunity to celebrate the holiday.

Blessed is the Eternal

    our God, ruler of the world,

    who made us holy by the mitzvot

    by commanding us
      to light the candles for the festival.

בָּרוּךְ אַתָּה יְיָ,
אֱלֹהֵינוּ מֶלֶךְ הָעוֹלָם,
אֲשֶׁר קִדְּשָׁנוּ בְּמִצְוֹתָיו,
וְצִוָּנוּ לְהַדְלִיק נֵר שֶׁל יוֹם טוֹב.

Blessed is the Eternal

    our God, ruler of the world,

    who kept us alive and well,

    and gave us the opportunity, to
      celebrate this occasion.

בָּרוּךְ אַתָּה יְיָ,
אֱלֹהֵינוּ מֶלֶךְ הָעוֹלָם,
שֶׁהֶחֱיָנוּ וְקִיְּמָנוּ
וְהִגִּיעָנוּ לַזְּמַן הַזֶּה.

PRAYER VOCABULARY

Pilgrimage Festivals	שָׁלֹשׁ רְגָלִים
Holiday	יוֹם טוֹב
Who kept us alive	שֶׁהֶחֱיָנוּ
This occasion	לַזְּמַן הַזֶּה

A special prayer of praise called Hallel is recited on the festivals. The prayer is made up of selections from different Psalms. The word Halleluyah, meaning "praise God," comes from the Hebrew word Hallel.

Psalm 113

Praise God.	הַלְלוּיָהּ.
Servants of God, praise the Almighty.	הַלְלוּ עַבְדֵי יְיָ.
Praise the name of the Almighty.	הַלְלוּ אֶת־שֵׁם יְיָ.
May God be praised now and forever.	יְהִי שֵׁם יְיָ מְבֹרָךְ, מֵעַתָּה וְעַד־עוֹלָם.
From the rising of the sun until it sets, God is to be praised.	מִמִּזְרַח־שֶׁמֶשׁ עַד־מְבוֹאוֹ, מְהֻלָּל שֵׁם יְיָ.
The Eternal is supreme above all nations.	רָם עַל־כָּל־גּוֹיִם יְיָ
God's glory is above the heavens.	עַל הַשָּׁמַיִם כְּבוֹדוֹ:
Who is like the Eternal, our God	מִי כַּיְיָ אֱלֹהֵינוּ
Enthroned so high,	הַמַּגְבִּיהִי לָשָׁבֶת:
Who looks down below	הַמַּשְׁפִּילִי לִרְאוֹת
Upon heaven and earth?	בַּשָּׁמַיִם וּבָאָרֶץ.
God raises the poor from the dust,	מְקִימִי מֵעָפָר דָּל,
the needy from the depths.	מֵאַשְׁפֹּת יָרִים אֶבְיוֹן.
Placing them among the princes of his people.	לְהוֹשִׁיבִי עִם־נְדִיבִים, עִם נְדִיבֵי עַמּוֹ.
The Almighty brings joy to the childless	מוֹשִׁיבִי עֲקֶרֶת הַבַּיִת,
by making them the parents of children.	אֵם־הַבָּנִים שְׂמֵחָה,
Praise God.	הַלְלוּיָהּ.

SERVANTS OF GOD, PRAISE THE ALMIGHTY   הַלְלוּ עַבְדֵי יְיָ

The hymn of praise known as Hallel comes from Psalms 113–118. Hallel is recited on Passover, Shavuot, and Sukkot. It is also recited on Chanukah and Rosh Chodesh.

Psalm 117

Let all nations praise God.	הַלְלוּ אֶת־יְיָ כָּל־גּוֹיִם.
Let all peoples glorify the Almighty.	שַׁבְּחוּהוּ כָּל־הָאֻמִּים.
Because God's kindness embraces us.	כִּי גָבַר עָלֵינוּ חַסְדּוֹ.
God's truth is forever. Halleluyah.	וֶאֱמֶת־יְיָ לְעוֹלָם, הַלְלוּיָהּ.

PRAYER VOCABULARY

Praise	הַלֵּל
Praise God	הַלְלוּיָהּ
Servants of God	עַבְדֵי יְיָ
Raising the poor from the dust	מְקִימִי מֵעָפָר דָּל
God's truth is forever	וֶאֱמֶת יְיָ לְעוֹלָם

As on all festive occasions, Kiddush is recited over a cup of wine as part of the celebration of each of the festivals. The Kiddush is the same for all the holidays except for a few "fill-in" words that tell which holiday is being celebrated and briefly describe the holiday. When the holiday begins on Shabbat, we start the Kiddush with the story of the first Shabbat from the Torah and continue with the regular holiday Kiddush.

If the holiday begins on Shabbat, start here and add the words in parentheses in the regular holiday Kiddush.

It was evening and morning on the sixth day.	וַיְהִי־עֶרֶב, וַיְהִי־בֹקֶר, יוֹם הַשִּׁשִּׁי.
The heavens and the earth and all that was within them had been completed.	וַיְכֻלּוּ הַשָּׁמַיִם וְהָאָרֶץ וְכָל־צְבָאָם.
God finished all the work of creation by the seventh day.	וַיְכַל אֱלֹהִים בַּיּוֹם הַשְּׁבִיעִי, מְלַאכְתּוֹ אֲשֶׁר עָשָׂה,
And God rested on the seventh day	וַיִּשְׁבֹּת בַּיּוֹם הַשְּׁבִיעִי,
from doing all the work of creation.	מִכָּל מְלַאכְתּוֹ אֲשֶׁר עָשָׂה.
And God blessed the seventh day	וַיְבָרֶךְ אֱלֹהִים אֶת־יוֹם הַשְּׁבִיעִי,
and made it holy,	וַיְקַדֵּשׁ אֹתוֹ,
because on it God had rested from	כִּי בוֹ שָׁבַת מִכָּל מְלַאכְתּוֹ,
all the work of creation.	אֲשֶׁר בָּרָא אֱלֹהִים לַעֲשׂוֹת.

Blessed is the Eternal

   our God, ruler of the world,

   who created the fruit of the vine.

בָּרוּךְ אַתָּה יְיָ,

אֱלֹהֵינוּ מֶלֶךְ הָעוֹלָם,

בּוֹרֵא פְּרִי הַגָּפֶן.

Blessed is the Eternal

   our God, ruler of the world,

   who chose us from among all nations

   and raised us from among all other
     peoples

   and made us holy with divine
     commandments,

and in love, gave us

   (Shabbats of rest

   festivals of joy

   and special days of gladness.

בָּרוּךְ אַתָּה יְיָ, אֱלֹהֵינוּ מֶלֶךְ הָעוֹלָם,

אֲשֶׁר בָּחַר בָּנוּ מִכָּל־עָם,

וְרוֹמְמָנוּ מִכָּל־לָשׁוֹן,

וְקִדְּשָׁנוּ בְּמִצְוֹתָיו.

וַתִּתֶּן־לָנוּ, יְיָ אֱלֹהֵינוּ, בְּאַהֲבָה,

(שַׁבָּתוֹת לִמְנוּחָה)

מוֹעֲדִים לְשִׂמְחָה,

חַגִּים וּזְמַנִּים לְשָׂשׂוֹן,

This holiday of   אֶת־יוֹם

**At each festival the appropriate Hebrew name is
inserted in the reading at this point:**

   the holiday of Matzot,

   the time of freedom.

חַג הַמַּצּוֹת הַזֶּה,

זְמַן חֵרוּתֵנוּ,

   the holiday of Shavuot,

the time of the giving of the Torah.

חַג הַשָּׁבוּעוֹת הַזֶּה,

זְמַן מַתַּן תּוֹרָתֵנוּ,

   the holiday of Sukkot,

   the time of joy.

חַג הַסֻּכּוֹת הַזֶּה,

זְמַן שִׂמְחָתֵנוּ,

the Festival of the Eighth Day,

   the time of joy.

הַשְּׁמִינִי חַג הָעֲצֶרֶת הַזֶּה,

זְמַן שִׂמְחָתֵנוּ,

God gave us (in love) this holy event, so that we may remember our exodus from Egypt.

(בְּאַהֲבָה) מִקְרָא קֹדֶשׁ,
זֵכֶר לִיצִיאַת מִצְרָיִם.

You have chosen us and made us holy among all the nations

כִּי בָנוּ בָחַרְתָּ, וְאוֹתָנוּ קִדַּשְׁתָּ,
מִכָּל הָעַמִּים.

And gave us Your holy days of joy (and your Shabbat with love).

(וְשַׁבָּת) וּמוֹעֲדֵי קָדְשֶׁךָ, (בְּאַהֲבָה וּבְרָצוֹן)
בְּשִׂמְחָה וּבְשָׂשׂוֹן הִנְחַלְתָּנוּ.

Blessed is God,

בָּרוּךְ אַתָּה יְיָ,

who makes holy (Shabbat),

מְקַדֵּשׁ (הַשַּׁבָּת, וְ)

Israel, and all the seasons.

יִשְׂרָאֵל וְהַזְּמַנִּים.

On the first days of each festival, add Shehecheyanu (p. 142).

PRAYER VOCABULARY	
Festivals of joy	מוֹעֲדִים לְשִׂמְחָה
And special days of gladness	חַגִּים וּזְמַנִּים לְשָׂשׂוֹן
The holiday of Matzot	חַג הַמַּצּוֹת
The time of freedom	זְמַן חֵרוּתֵנוּ
The Festival of Shavuot	שָׁבוּעוֹת
The time of the giving of the Torah	זְמַן מַתַּן תּוֹרָתֵנוּ
The holiday of Sukkot	סֻכּוֹת
The festival of the eighth day	שְׁמִינִי עֲצֶרֶת
You made us holy	אוֹתָנוּ קִדַּשְׁתָּ,
Your holy days of joy	מוֹעֲדֵי קָדְשֶׁךָ

157

SUKKOT סֻכּוֹת

The festival of Sukkot, which follows the solemn days of Rosh Hashanah and Yom Kippur, is both an agricultural and a historical holiday. It recalls the fruit harvest of ancient days as well as the wanderings of the Jews in the desert after they left Egypt. We build a temporary shelter called a sukkah to remind us of the temporary shelters built by the Jews as wanderers in the desert, and we bless the lulav and etrog to commemorate the agricultural aspect of the holiday.

PRAYER VOCABULARY

The Festival of Sukkot (Booths)	סֻכּוֹת
Rosh Hashanah	רֹאשׁ הַשָּׁנָה
Yom Kippur	יוֹם כִּפּוּר
Egypt	מִצְרַיִם
Sukkah (Sukkot)	סֻכָּה (סֻכּוֹת)
Lulav	לוּלָב
Etrog	אֶתְרוֹג

On Sukkot we build a little booth or hut called a Suk-kah. It reminds us of the time the Jews built temporary shelters when they lived as wanderers in the desert. We say a special prayer in the Sukkah before eating bread or cake.

Blessed is the Eternal

בָּרוּךְ אַתָּה יְיָ,

    our God, ruler of the world,

אֱלֹהֵינוּ מֶלֶךְ הָעוֹלָם,

    who made us holy by the mitzvot

אֲשֶׁר קִדְּשָׁנוּ בְּמִצְוֹתָיו

    and commanded us to stay in the Sukkah.

וְצִוָּנוּ לֵישֵׁב בַּסֻּכָּה.

To stay in the Sukkah   לֵישֵׁב בַּסֻּכָּה

The lulav and the etrog remind us that once the Jews were farmers in the land of Israel and that many of the symbols and rituals of the holidays go back to that agricultural period. The following blessing is said as we wave the lulav and smell the sweet aroma of the etrog.

Blessed is the Eternal,

    our God, ruler of the world,

    who gave us divine
        commandments to make us holy,

    and commanded us to wave the
        lulav.

בָּרוּךְ אַתָּה יְיָ,

אֱלֹהֵינוּ מֶלֶךְ הָעוֹלָם,

אֲשֶׁר קִדְּשָׁנוּ בְּמִצְוֹתָיו,

וְצִוָּנוּ עַל נְטִילַת לוּלָב.

PRAYER VOCABULARY

To wave the lulav	עַל נְטִילַת לוּלָב
Palm branch	לוּלָב
Citron	אֶתְרוֹג
Willow	עֲרָבָה
Myrtle	הֲדַס

SHEMINI ATZERET AND SIMCHAT TORAH!

שִׂמְחַת תּוֹרָה   שְׁמִינִי עֲצֶרֶת

In the Bible, the last day of the eight-day festival of Sukkot is called Shemini Atzeret, which means "the eighth day of solemn assembly." Although the original purpose and meaning of this day is uncertain, it is believed that it was related in some way to an aspect of the harvest.

The Day after Shemini Atzeret is Simchat Torah, the day of rejoicing that marks the end of the Torah reading cycle, and the beginning of the cycle of the next year.

The service on Simchat Torah is the most joyous of the entire year. In many synagogues, the members of the congregation dance and sing as they carry the Torahs around the sanctuary in a happy procession. Children follow behind carrying flags topped with apples and sometimes with candles. The procession, known as *hakafot*, circles the synagogue seven times. Each time different people carry the scrolls until everyone has had a chance to carry a Torah.

When the Torah reading has been completed and the service is ended, refreshments are served. This ends the fall holiday season which began so solemnly with the observance of Rosh Hashanah.

The symbolism of the day is clear. The cycle of Torah readings for the year has been completed, but the Torah's role in our lives never ends. It is always there to teach us new things and give us new insights. So as soon as we complete the last Sidra, we start anew with the first.

אָנָּא יְיָ לִי

This prayer is recited during the Torah reading
ceremony on Shemini Atzeret—Simchat Torah.

We pray, O Eternal, save us.	אָנָּא יְיָ הוֹשִׁיעָה נָּא.
We pray, O Eternal, let us prosper.	אָנָּא יְיָ הַצְלִיחָה נָא:
O Eternal, answer us when we call.	אָנָּא יְיָ עֲנֵנוּ בְיוֹם קָרְאֵנוּ:

שִׂישׂוּ וְשִׂמְחוּ

Simchat Torah is a time for rejoicing. This happy song
is sung during the Hakafot procession.

Be happy!	שִׂישׂוּ וְשִׂמְחוּ
It's Simchat Torah.	בְּשִׂמְחַת תּוֹרָה,
Honor the Torah.	וּתְנוּ כָבוֹד לַתּוֹרָה.
Rejoice with this Torah	נָגִיל וְנָשִׂישׂ בְּזֹאת הַתּוֹרָה,
Because it is our strength and our light.	כִּי הִיא לָנוּ עֹז וְאוֹרָה.

PRAYER VOCABULARY	
Save us	הוֹשִׁיעָה נָּא
Be happy!	שִׂישׂוּ וְשִׂמְחוּ
Our strength and our light	עֹז וְאוֹרָה

The festival of Passover is celebrated at home by having a family Seder. This ritual is so named because it follows a set "order." One of the highlights of the evening is the asking of the Four Questions by the youngest child.

PRAYER VOCABULARY

Passover	פֶּסַח
Seder	סֵדֶר
Four Questions	אַרְבַּע קֻשִׁיּוֹת

The Four Questions, as well as the rest of the Seder ritual, are found in the Haggadah, a special book which has the order of the service and all the prayers, readings, and songs associated with the Seder.

Why is this night different from all other nights?

מַה נִּשְׁתַּנָּה הַלַּיְלָה הַזֶּה מִכָּל הַלֵּילוֹת?

1. On all other nights we eat leavened bread or matzah.

   On this night only matzah.

1. שֶׁבְּכָל הַלֵּילוֹת אָנוּ אוֹכְלִין חָמֵץ וּמַצָּה,
   הַלַּיְלָה הַזֶּה כֻּלּוֹ מַצָּה.

2. On all other nights we eat all kinds of herbs.

   On this night, bitter herbs.

2. שֶׁבְּכָל הַלֵּילוֹת אָנוּ אוֹכְלִין שְׁאָר יְרָקוֹת,
   הַלַּיְלָה הַזֶּה מָרוֹר.

3. On all other nights we do not dip even once.

   On this night, twice.

3. שֶׁבְּכָל הַלֵּילוֹת אֵין אָנוּ מַטְבִּילִין אֲפִילוּ פַּעַם אֶחָת,
   הַלַּיְלָה הַזֶּה שְׁתֵּי פְעָמִים.

4. On all other nights we do not eat with special ceremony.

   On this night we all eat in a festive manner.

4. שֶׁבְּכָל הַלֵּילוֹת אָנוּ אוֹכְלִין בֵּין יוֹשְׁבִין וּבֵין מְסֻבִּין,
   הַלַּיְלָה הַזֶּה כֻּלָּנוּ מְסֻבִּין.

WHY IS THIS NIGHT DIFFERENT? מַה נִּשְׁתַּנָּה הַלַּיְלָה הַזֶּה

The Four Questions ask "Why is this night different?" The answer is contained in the story of the departure from Egypt told in the Haggadah. This night is different because on it we remember that *we* were slaves and *we* were freed from Egypt. We are told that all of us are to think of ourselves as if we ourselves were slaves and were freed from slavery.

PRAYER VOCABULARY	
The four questions	אַרְבַּע קֻשְׁיוֹת
Why is this night different	מַה נִּשְׁתַּנָּה הַלַּיְלָה הַזֶּה
On all other nights	שֶׁבְּכָל הַלֵּילוֹת
Only matzah	כֻּלּוֹ מַצָּה
All kinds of herbs	שְׁאָר יְרָקוֹת
Bitter herbs	מָרוֹר
We do not dip even once	אֵין אָנוּ מַטְבִּילִין אֲפִילוּ פַּעַם אֶחָת
Twice	שְׁתֵּי פְעָמִים

עֲבָדִים הָיִינוּ

The Haggadah tells the story of the exodus from slavery in Egypt to freedom. This is how the dramatic story begins.

Once, we were Pharaoh's slaves in Egypt.	עֲבָדִים הָיִינוּ לְפַרְעֹה בְּמִצְרַיִם,
And the Eternal our God took us out of there	וַיּוֹצִיאֵנוּ יְיָ אֱלֹהֵינוּ מִשָּׁם,
with a strong hand and an outstretched arm.	בְּיָד חֲזָקָה וּבִזְרֹעַ נְטוּיָה.

The next four blessings are an important part of the Seder ritual.

Before we eat the Karpas we say:

Blessed is the Eternal
   our God, ruler of the world,
   who created produce of the soil.

בָּרוּךְ אַתָּה יְיָ, אֱלֹהֵינוּ מֶלֶךְ הָעוֹלָם,

בּוֹרֵא פְּרִי הָאֲדָמָה.

Before we eat the Matzah we say:

Blessed is the Eternal
   our God, ruler of the world,

   who brings forth food
   from the earth.

בָּרוּךְ אַתָּה יְיָ, אֱלֹהֵינוּ מֶלֶךְ הָעוֹלָם,

הַמּוֹצִיא לֶחֶם מִן הָאָרֶץ.

Blessed is the Eternal
   our God, ruler of the world,

   who made us holy by the mitzvot

   and commanded us to eat matzah.

בָּרוּךְ אַתָּה יְיָ, אֱלֹהֵינוּ מֶלֶךְ הָעוֹלָם,

אֲשֶׁר קִדְּשָׁנוּ בְּמִצְוֹתָיו,

וְצִוָּנוּ עַל אֲכִילַת מַצָּה.

Before we eat the Maror we say:

Blessed is the Eternal
   our God, ruler of the world,

   who made us holy by the mitzvot

   and commanded us to eat bitter
   herbs.

בָּרוּךְ אַתָּה יְיָ, אֱלֹהֵינוּ מֶלֶךְ הָעוֹלָם,

אֲשֶׁר קִדְּשָׁנוּ בְּמִצְוֹתָיו,

וְצִוָּנוּ עַל אֲכִילַת מָרוֹר.

PRAYER VOCABULARY	
Produce of the soil	פְּרִי הָאֲדָמָה
The eating of matzah	עַל אֲכִילַת מַצָּה
Bitter herbs	מָרוֹר

SHAVUOT שָׁבוּעוֹת

The Torah is the center of Jewish life. It contains our religious laws and traditions, and has been a guide for Jewish conduct through the ages. According to tradition, Moses received the Torah from God on Mount Sinai as the Israelites waited at the foot of the mountain. Shavuot commemorates this important religious experience. But like the other festivals, it has an agricultural significance as well. It was the season of the barley harvest.

PRAYER VOCABULARY

Torah	תּוֹרָה
Mount Sinai	הַר סִינַי

Shavuot, which is celebrated seven weeks after Passover, is important to Reform Jews as the day of Confirmation. As part of the ceremony, the boys and girls who are being confirmed read or recite the Ten Commandments as a symbol of their dedication to the ideals of Torah.

God spoke all these words saying:

וַיְדַבֵּר אֱלֹהִים אֵת כָּל־הַדְּבָרִים הָאֵלֶּה לֵאמֹר:

1. I am the Eternal your God,

1. אָנֹכִי יְיָ אֱלֹהֶיךָ,

who brought you out of the land of Egypt, out of the house of slavery.

אֲשֶׁר הוֹצֵאתִיךָ מֵאֶרֶץ מִצְרַיִם מִבֵּית עֲבָדִים.

2. You shall have no other gods besides Me.

2. לֹא־יִהְיֶה לְךָ אֱלֹהִים אֲחֵרִים עַל־פָּנָי.

You shall not make yourself an idol

לֹא־תַעֲשֶׂה לְךָ פֶסֶל

or any likeness of anything that is in the heavens above,

וְכָל־תְּמוּנָה אֲשֶׁר בַּשָּׁמַיִם

or that is on the earth below,

מִמַּעַל, וַאֲשֶׁר בָּאָרֶץ מִתַּחַת,

or that is in the waters under the earth;

וַאֲשֶׁר בַּמַּיִם מִתַּחַת לָאָרֶץ.

You shall not bow down to them or serve them;

לֹא־תִשְׁתַּחֲוֶה לָהֶם וְלֹא תָעָבְדֵם,

for I the Eternal your God am a jealous God,

כִּי אָנֹכִי יְיָ אֱלֹהֶיךָ, אֵל קַנָּא,

visiting the sins of the fathers upon the children to the third

פֹּקֵד עֲוֹן אָבֹת עַל־בָּנִים, עַל־שִׁלֵּשִׁים

and fourth generation of those who hate Me,

וְעַל־רִבֵּעִים לְשֹׂנְאָי.

but showing lovingkindness to thousands

וְעֹשֶׂה חֶסֶד לַאֲלָפִים,

of those who love Me and keep My mitzvot.

לְאֹהֲבַי, וּלְשֹׁמְרֵי מִצְוֹתָי.

You shall not take the name of the
Eternal your God in vain;

   for the Eternal will not hold them
   guiltless who take the holy name
   in vain.

Remember Shabbat, to keep it holy.

Six days you shall labor,

   and do all your work;

but the seventh day is a Sabbath

   to the Eternal your God:

on it you shall not do any work,

   you, or your son, or your daughter,

   your manservant or your
   maidservant,

   or your cattle, or the stranger who
   is within your gates;

   for in six days the Eternal made the
   heavens
      and the earth, the sea,
      and all that is in them,

   and rested on the seventh day:

   therefore the Eternal blessed the
   Shabbat day and made it holy.

Honor your father and mother,

   that your days may be long on the
   land

   which the Eternal your God gives you.

3 לֹא תִשָּׂא אֶת־שֵׁם־יְיָ אֱלֹהֶיךָ לַשָּׁוְא,

כִּי לֹא יְנַקֶּה יְיָ אֵת אֲשֶׁר־יִשָּׂא אֶת־
שְׁמוֹ לַשָּׁוְא.

4 זָכוֹר אֶת־יוֹם הַשַּׁבָּת לְקַדְּשׁוֹ.
שֵׁשֶׁת יָמִים תַּעֲבֹד
וְעָשִׂיתָ כָּל־מְלַאכְתֶּךָ.
וְיוֹם הַשְּׁבִיעִי, שַׁבָּת
לַיְיָ אֱלֹהֶיךָ.
לֹא־תַעֲשֶׂה כָל־מְלָאכָה,
אַתָּה, וּבִנְךָ־וּבִתֶּךָ,
עַבְדְּךָ וַאֲמָתֶךָ,
וּבְהֶמְתֶּךָ, וְגֵרְךָ אֲשֶׁר בִּשְׁעָרֶיךָ,
כִּי שֵׁשֶׁת־יָמִים עָשָׂה יְיָ אֶת־הַשָּׁמַיִם
וְאֶת־הָאָרֶץ, אֶת־הַיָּם וְאֶת־כָּל־אֲשֶׁר־
בָּם,
וַיָּנַח בַּיּוֹם הַשְּׁבִיעִי,
עַל־כֵּן, בֵּרַךְ יְיָ אֶת־יוֹם הַשַּׁבָּת
וַיְקַדְּשֵׁהוּ.

5 כַּבֵּד אֶת־אָבִיךָ וְאֶת־אִמֶּךָ,
לְמַעַן יַאֲרִכוּן יָמֶיךָ, עַל הָאֲדָמָה
אֲשֶׁר־יְיָ אֱלֹהֶיךָ נֹתֵן לָךְ.

You shall not murder.	6 לֹא תִּרְצָח.
You shall not commit adultery.	7 לֹא תִּנְאָף.
You shall not steal.	8 לֹא תִּגְנֹב.
You shall not bear false witness against your neighbor.	9 לֹא־תַעֲנֶה בְרֵעֲךָ עֵד שָׁקֶר.
You shall not covet your neighbor's house;	10 לֹא תַחְמֹד בֵּית רֵעֶךָ.

לֹא תַחְמֹד אֵשֶׁת רֵעֶךָ,

וְעַבְדּוֹ וַאֲמָתוֹ, וְשׁוֹרוֹ וַחֲמֹרוֹ, וְכֹל

אֲשֶׁר לְרֵעֶךָ.

You shall not covet your neighbor's wife.
You shall not envy your neighbor his servants, animals, nor anything which belongs to him.

PRAYER VOCABULARY

Weeks	שָׁבוּעוֹת
The Ten Commandments	עֲשֶׂרֶת הַדִּבְּרוֹת
Out of the house of slavery	מִבֵּית עֲבָדִים
But showing lovingkindness	וְעֹשֶׂה חֶסֶד
Remember Shabbat	זָכוֹר אֶת יוֹם הַשַּׁבָּת
Six days you shall labor	שֵׁשֶׁת יָמִים תַּעֲבֹד
You shall not do any work	לֹא־תַעֲשֶׂה כָל־מְלָאכָה,
And made it holy	וַיְקַדְּשֵׁהוּ
Honor your father and mother	כַּבֵּד אֶת אָבִיךָ וְאֶת אִמֶּךָ
You shall not murder	לֹא תִּרְצָח
You shall not steal	לֹא תִּגְנֹב
You shall not bear false witness against your neighbor	לֹא תַעֲנֶה בְרֵעֲךָ עֵד שָׁקֶר
You shall not covet your neighbor's house	לֹא תַחְמֹד בֵּית רֵעֶךָ

171

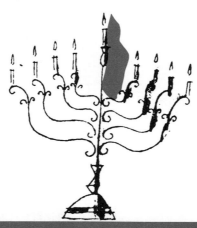

CHANUKAH   חֲנוּכָּה

Chanukah is a very recent holiday as Jewish holidays go. It dates back to 165 B.C.E., when a small band of Jewish freedom fighters under the command of Judah Maccabee defeated the mighty armies of Syria and won for the Jews the right to worship God according to the rules and traditions of Judaism. They rededicated the Holy Temple which had been defiled and relit its oil Menorah. Chanukah is celebrated by lighting the menorah (or Chanukiyah). One candle is added each day until, on the eighth day, eight candles are lit. There is also much singing, dancing, eating of latkes, and giving of presents, especially to the children.

PRAYER VOCABULARY

Chanukah (rededication)	חֲנוּכָּה
Judah Maccabee	יְהוּדָה מַכַּבִּי
Latkes	לְבִיבוֹת
Chanukah menorah	חֲנוּכִּיָה

הַדְלָקַת הַנֵּרוֹת שֶׁל חֲנֻכָּה

Candles are lit on the eight nights of Chanukah in an eight-branched menorah called a Chanukiyah. The following blessings are said:

Blessed is the Eternal

our God, ruler of the world,
בָּרוּךְ אַתָּה יְיָ, אֱלֹהֵינוּ מֶלֶךְ הָעוֹלָם,

who made us holy by the mitzvot
אֲשֶׁר קִדְּשָׁנוּ בְּמִצְוֹתָיו,

and commanded us to light Chanukah candles.
וְצִוָּנוּ לְהַדְלִיק נֵר שֶׁל חֲנֻכָּה.

Blessed is the Eternal

our God, ruler of the world,
בָּרוּךְ אַתָּה יְיָ, אֱלֹהֵינוּ מֶלֶךְ הָעוֹלָם,

who did wonderful things for our ancestors
שֶׁעָשָׂה נִסִּים לַאֲבוֹתֵינוּ,

in those days, at this season.
בַּיָּמִים הָהֵם בַּזְּמַן הַזֶּה.

On the first night, the Shehecheyanu is added:

Blessed is the Eternal

our God, ruler of the world,
בָּרוּךְ אַתָּה יְיָ, אֱלֹהֵינוּ מֶלֶךְ הָעוֹלָם,

who kept us alive and well,
שֶׁהֶחֱיָנוּ, וְקִיְּמָנוּ,

and gave us the opportunity to celebrate this occasion.
וְהִגִּיעָנוּ לַזְּמַן הַזֶּה.

PRAYER VOCABULARY

Chanukah menorah	חֲנוּכִּיָּה
Chanukah candles	נֵרוֹת חֲנוּכָּה
Dedication	חֲנֻכָּה
Who did wonderful things	שֶׁעָשָׂה נִסִּים
In those days	בַּיָּמִים הָהֵם

PURIM   פּוּרִים

Although Purim seems to be a holiday created for having fun, dressing up in costume, and eating hamantaschen, it really has a serious message. When we recall the story of Purim in the Megillah, we are expressing our confidence that just as Haman, the cruel enemy of the Jews, met his deserved end, so too will all enemies of the Jews be overcome. We also admire the courage of the heroine, Esther, and her uncle, Mordechai, who saved the Jewish people in their generation.

PRAYER VOCABULARY

Feast of Lots	פּוּרִים
Hamantaschen	אָזְנֵי הָמָן
Scroll of Esther	מְגִלָּה
Haman	הָמָן
Jews	יְהוּדִים

On Purim we read the Megillah, the Scroll of Esther, with great joy and merrymaking. The following blessings are recited before the reading:

Blessed is the Eternal

    our God, ruler of the world,

    who made us holy by the mitzvot

    and commanded us to read the Megillah.

בָּרוּךְ אַתָּה יְיָ, אֱלֹהֵינוּ מֶלֶךְ הָעוֹלָם,

אֲשֶׁר קִדְּשָׁנוּ בְּמִצְוֹתָיו,

וְצִוָּנוּ עַל מִקְרָא מְגִלָּה.

Blessed is the Eternal

    our God, ruler of the world,

    who did wonderful things for our ancestors,

    in those days, at this season.

בָּרוּךְ אַתָּה יְיָ, אֱלֹהֵינוּ מֶלֶךְ הָעוֹלָם,

שֶׁעָשָׂה נִסִּים לַאֲבוֹתֵינוּ,

בַּיָּמִים הָהֵם בַּזְּמַן הַזֶּה.

Blessed is the Eternal

    our God, ruler of the world,
    who kept us alive and well, and

    gave us the opportunity to celebrate this occasion.

בָּרוּךְ אַתָּה יְיָ, אֱלֹהֵינוּ מֶלֶךְ הָעוֹלָם,

שֶׁהֶחֱיָנוּ, וְקִיְּמָנוּ,

וְהִגִּיעָנוּ לַזְּמַן הַזֶּה.

PRAYER VOCABULARY

Casting of lots	פּוּרִים
Scroll	מְגִלָּה
Scroll of Esther	מְגִלַּת אֶסְתֵּר
The reading of the Megillah	עַל מִקְרָא מְגִלָּה

מְגִלַּת אֶסְתֵּר

The Megillah reading begins with these verses:

It came to pass in the days of Ahasuerus,	וַיְהִי בִּימֵי אֲחַשְׁוֵרוֹשׁ,
the Ahasuerus who reigned from India to Ethiopia	הוּא אֲחַשְׁוֵרוֹשׁ, הַמֶּלֶךְ מֵהֹדּוּ וְעַד־כּוּשׁ,
over one hundred and twenty-seven provinces.	שֶׁבַע וְעֶשְׂרִים וּמֵאָה מְדִינָה.
In those days King Ahasuerus sat on his royal throne	בַּיָּמִים הָהֵם, כְּשֶׁבֶת הַמֶּלֶךְ אֲחַשְׁוֵרוֹשׁ עַל כִּסֵּא מַלְכוּתוֹ
in Shushan the capital.	אֲשֶׁר בְּשׁוּשַׁן הַבִּירָה.

PRAYER VOCABULARY	
It came to pass in the days of Ahasuerus	וַיְהִי בִּימֵי אֲחַשְׁוֵרוֹשׁ
His royal throne	כִּסֵּא מַלְכוּתוֹ
The capital·	הַבִּירָה

YOM HAATZMAUT   יוֹם הָעַצְמָאוּת

Throughout their history the Jews have loved the land of Israel. For almost two thousand years after 70 C.E., when they were driven from it, they longed to return. Finally, in 1948, the State of Israel was declared. This important event is commemorated as Yom Haatzmaut, Israeli Independence Day, in synagogues throughout the world. As part of their observance of Yom Haatzmaut, Conservative congregations recite a special Al Hanissim prayer in honor of the founding of the State of Israel.

PRAYER VOCABULARY

Israel	יִשְׂרָאֵל
The State of Israel	מְדִינַת יִשְׂרָאֵל
Israel Independence Day	יוֹם הָעַצְמָאוּת

The following hymn expresses the strong feelings Jews have always had for Jerusalem, the city in which the Bet Hamikdash once stood.

From the peak of Mount Scopus,	מֵעַל פִּסְגַּת הַר הַצּוֹפִים,
Shalom to you, Jerusalem.	שָׁלוֹם לָךְ, יְרוּשָׁלַיִם.
I have dreamed about you for a hundred generations,	מֵאָה דוֹרוֹת חָלַמְתִּי עָלַיִךְ
to be privileged to see your light.	לִזְכּוֹת לִרְאוֹת בְּאוֹר פָּנָיִךְ.
Jerusalem, Jerusalem,	יְרוּשָׁלַיִם, יְרוּשָׁלַיִם!
may your light shine upon your child.	הָאִירִי פָּנַיִךְ לִבְנֵךְ!
Jerusalem, Jerusalem,	יְרוּשָׁלַיִם, יְרוּשָׁלַיִם!
I will rebuild your ruins.	מֵחָרְבוֹתַיִךְ אֶבְנֵךְ!

PRAYER VOCABULARY

From the peak	מֵעַל פִּסְגַּת
I have dreamed about you	חָלַמְתִּי עָלַיִךְ
A hundred generations	מֵאָה דוֹרוֹת
I will rebuild your ruins	מֵחָרְבוֹתַיִךְ אֶבְנֵךְ

TISHA B'AV   תִּשְׁעָה בְּאָב

Tisha B'Av (The ninth of Av) is a day of mourning commemorating the destruction of the First Bet Hamikdash (Temple) in the year 586 B.C.E. and the Second Bet Hamikdash as well in 70. On this day the Jews were expelled from Spain in 1492.

Tisha B'Av occurs in the summertime. It is a fast day on which we recite Lamentations while sitting on the ground.

How lonely sits the city of Jerusalem once full of people!	אֵיכָה יָשְׁבָה בָדָד
This city which was once the greatest of all lies abandoned.	הָעִיר רַבָּתִי עָם הָיְתָה כְּאַלְמָנָה רַבָּתִי בַגּוֹיִם
The princess among states is now taken into captivity.	שָׂרָתִי בַּמְּדִינוֹת הָיְתָה לָמַס:
Turn us towards You, O Eternal, and we shall return to You.	הֲשִׁיבֵנוּ יְיָ אֵלֶיךָ וְנָשׁוּבָה
Renew our days as of old.	חַדֵּשׁ יָמֵינוּ כְּקֶדֶם:

HOW LONELY
אֵיכָה יָשְׁבָה בָדָד

According to tradition, the book of Lamentations was written by the prophet Jeremiah who witnessed the destruction of the First Temple. He describes the once great city with its magnificent Holy Temple now reduced to lonely ruins and rubble. We pray that after this great tragedy, God will show us the way to return to the life of mitzvot, and we shall be restored as a people and returned to our land.

PRAYER VOCABULARY

City	עִיר
Full of people	רַבָּתִי עָם
Turn us toward You, O Eternal	הֲשִׁיבֵנוּ יְיָ אֵלֶיךָ

YOM HASHOAH   יוֹם הַשׁוֹאָה

This day commemorates the saddest period in Jewish history, the Holocaust, when six million Jews were murdered, wiping out many of the Jewish communities of Europe. Many congregations mark this day in spring with prayers. Yom Hashoah services usually include the recitation of Kaddish and the lighting of memorial candles for the six million martyrs.

PRAYER VOCABULARY

Day of the Holocaust	יוֹם הַשׁוֹאָה

181

אֲנִי מַאֲמִין

Special services are held in many synagogues on Yom Hashoah. One of the prayers recited is Ani Maamin, which expresses faith in God and in a Messianic Age of Peace no matter what happens.

I believe with complete faith in the coming of the Messiah	אֲנִי מַאֲמִין בֶּאֱמוּנָה שְׁלֵמָה בְּבִיאַת הַמָּשִׁיחַ.
And though he takes a long time to arrive	וְאַף עַל פִּי שֶׁיִּתְמַהְמֵהַּ,
Even so, I still will wait for him.	עִם כָּל־זֶה אֲחַכֶּה לוֹ
Each day until he comes.	בְּכָל־יוֹם שֶׁיָּבֹא.